CALL
OF THE
KINGFISHER

BRIGHT SIGHTS AND BIRDSONG IN
A YEAR BY THE RIVER

NICK PENNY

CALL

OF THE

KINGFISHER

BRIGHT SIGHTS AND BIRDSONG IN
A YEAR BY THE RIVER

NICK PENNY

First published in the UK in July 2023 by
Bradt Guides Ltd
31a High Street, Chesham, HP5 1BW, England
www.bradtguides.com

Print edition published in the USA by The Globe Pequot Press Inc,
PO Box 480, Guilford, Connecticut 06437-0480

Edited and project-managed by James Lowen
Cover design and illustrations by Jasmine Parker
Layout and typesetting by Ian Spick, Bradt Guides
Production-managed by Sue Cooper

ISBN: 9781804691113

British Library Cataloguing in Publication Data
A catalogue record for this book is available from the British Library

Digital conversion by www.dataworks.co.in
Printed in the UK by Jellyfish Print Solutions.

That kingfisher jewelling upstream
seems to leave a streak of itself
in the bright air. The trees
are all the better for its passing.

from *Kingfisher*, by Norman MacCaig

AUDIO MATERIAL

The text of *Call of the Kingfisher* is complemented by a bonus suite of recordings of birds and other wildlife which readers may listen to online. Indicated by a speaker icon (◀)), these are numbered individually and placed at appropriate points in each chapter. To listen while reading, simply scan the QR code below (or visit www.bradtguides.com/call-of-the-kingfisher-audio-recordings on your browser) to access the relevant page on the Bradt Travel Guides website. Then scroll down to the chapter you are reading and click on the numbered recording.

AUTHOR

Nick Penny (nickpenny.com) grew up in different parts of the world before doing an arts degree at Oxford University. He then set up his own workshop making musical instruments, as well as writing music and playing the Paraguayan harp. After moving to rural Northamptonshire he became fascinated by the birdsong in his local woods and started recording the sounds to use in his own music. Nick also began to watch and photograph the kingfishers on the River Nene close to his home – experiences captured in his nature-writing debut, *Call of the Kingfisher*.

CONTENTS

INTRODUCTION

This book is a love letter to a short stretch of the River Nene a little over a mile long between Oundle and Cotterstock in Northamptonshire. That love extends to all the wild things that live there, and especially the kingfishers.

I've walked the riverside path for over three decades. If I'm just doing it for the exercise, or time is short, I can easily get to Cotterstock and be back home again in an hour. But for a whole year I gave the river all the time it asked for. Often that might be a morning, but sometimes in spring I spent nearly every waking hour there. I didn't want to miss a thing.

The more I walked the path, and the more attention I gave it, the more I saw and heard the kingfishers. If I didn't see one the walk could still be lovely, but the sight of that glorious flash of light and colour always made my day. It was like finding both the rainbow and the pot of gold at the same time.

So this is a book about a year by the river and my experiences while passing through it. Other strands are woven in. There are trips to local woods to listen to nightingales, and visits to other times and places in the Nene valley and beyond. There are also the stories of a surprising number of naturalists and nature writers who once lived and worked in the area. But the background tapestry is the sights and sounds and greens and browns of the riverbank, shot through with the blue and orange threads of a kingfisher's glowing feathers.

JANUARY

1 JANUARY: There's magic in the meadows this morning. I'm standing on the bridge across the river, listening to the echoing calls of robins and great tits. A low sun breaks through the mist. It creates little pockets of light in the willow trees on the far bank. I glance down as a slight movement catches my eye. There's a tiny shape on a post at the water's edge. It's hardly bigger than a sparrow. From this distance all I can see is a rounded scrap of orange that could easily be mistaken for a robin's red breast. Then it turns, and the sun picks out the royal blue of a kingfisher's wings. It turns again, and the bright azure stripe down its back shimmers like a sunlit stream.

I can just make out the profile of the head and beak as it searches for small fish that swim into the backwaters to escape the swirl of the river. It makes a little bobbing movement then dives in with a barely audible splash and returns with a minnow. Then it swallows it whole, lets out a high, piping '*tzee!*', and streaks off across the water till it's out of sight.

I was fourteen when I first saw a dazzling blue shape flash past and disappear upriver. It was so bright it looked like it was lit up from inside. I was walking on my own, and the sheer surprise of it left me dumbstruck. For a few moments I could barely breathe or think. It took a while before the word 'kingfisher' swam into my mind. Even now, each encounter with one brings a sense of wonder and a feeling of being blessed.

I start to walk further along the bridge. It's a long stone causeway that lifts the road above the floodplain for hundreds of yards before crossing the River Nene. There have been a few weeks of heavy rain, and flocks of gulls and geese bob about on the floods that have drowned parts of the meadow on either side. To the east there are open fields, but for four centuries it was the site of a substantial Roman settlement. It was a major centre for ironworking. I imagine the smoke from wood and charcoal fires drifting towards the river, and the distant sounds of hammering. More recently, during the 1980s, I'd sometimes catch a whiff of burnt biscuit from the chimney of the sugar beet factory in Peterborough twelve miles away.

Now I'm standing right above the main river. I can hear it rushing through the stone arches beneath me. The small market town of Oundle, where I live, is about halfway along the hundred-mile journey it makes from its source in southwest Northamptonshire to the Wash estuary and the North Sea. From here I can see the river snaking off downstream through the meadows towards the gentle wooded hills around the village of Southwick. Then it turns northeast towards the village of Cotterstock and passes in front of a tall, sloping wood of ash and willow trees that curls along the horizon like a long leaf laid on its side.

Usually I'd go down to the riverbank and walk straight into this landscape. But the paths are flooded. Instead, I'm hatching a plan. I've lived and walked here for decades, and occasionally see kingfishers, but large parts of their lives are a mystery to me. Spotting one on the first day of the year seems like a sign. After a busy life as a musician I've reached an age and stage where I'm freer to pick and choose how to use my time. Why not spend a year looking out for them, keeping a journal, reading the literature and learning as much as I can?

I've no idea whether they'll be on this stretch of the river throughout the year, or if I'll see enough of them to get a complete picture. But there'll be plenty of other things to watch and listen to, both here and in the surrounding countryside. There are woods not far away with rare butterflies, little owls and nightingales. The time won't be wasted. I walk back across the bridge, back to my own front door just a few minutes away, excited by the challenges and hoping for surprises. Who knows what the new year might bring?

2 JANUARY: I've been looking through some books and articles, and the bird I saw yesterday is known as a common kingfisher. Its Latin name is *Alcedo atthis*, and it's one of over a hundred different species of kingfisher found across the world. It's the only member of the family that lives and breeds here in the UK, but is widespread in many parts of Europe and Asia. While I was marvelling at those beautiful shining feathers someone could have been sharing the same thoughts in India or Japan.

I walk down to the bridge and for the second day in a row I can see a soft round shape perched near the water. This time it's crouched and barely showing through the jagged twigs and brambles in a hawthorn bush. I have my camera with me, so I look through the viewfinder and zoom in. It's impossible not to smile at the sight of those glorious iridescent feathers. There's a distinctive orange colouring on the lower bill which means she's a female (a 'queenfisher'?). If it was a male the beak would be uniformly dark. Today's light brings out a bright green tinge in her blue feathers.

From her perch just above the water she makes a couple of short dives, sending tiny ripples across the surface, before returning to the same branch to preen her feathers. Then she takes off, flying directly towards the part of the bridge where I'm standing. There's an arch right below me, so when she disappears, I guess she's flown through to the other side. But some instinct makes me move closer to the parapet and peer directly down at some corroded metal brackets that stick up out of the channel that runs alongside the bridge. They once had thick planks fixed to them to make a jetty, but the wood's rotted away, leaving a row of long, upright metal bolts. And there she is, perched on the head of a bolt, just yards away. She's still for an instant, then senses my presence and is gone.

I step back from the parapet. Right next to me there's an inscription carved into a block of stone:

IN THE YERE OF OVRE LORD 1570
THES ARCHES WER BORN DOVNE BY
THE WATERS EXTREMITIE
IN THE YERE OF OVRE LORD 1571
THEY WER BVILDED AGAYN
WITH LIME AND STONNE

The current floods are fairly high, but the modern river's been tamed by locks and weirs and the bridge isn't in danger. As I look out across the meadows there are more patches of green showing, and the water levels are slowly going down. In a couple of days it should be fine to walk there again.

4 JANUARY: At last it's safe to walk along the riverbank, but it's a nippy morning with a strong northeasterly. There's no mercy in a wind from that direction. It howls across from Peterborough and the Fens and whacks you full in the face.

I'm walking with the river to my left, on the slightly raised bank formed by mud being dredged from the riverbed and dumped to the sides. It's narrow enough here to shout "good morning" to someone walking on the other side of the river, but too wide to have a proper conversation. The meadows on the far side are rough and occasionally grazed by cattle. At the downstream end is Snipe Meadow, a small nature reserve maintained as an old-fashioned water meadow. The meadows on this side are used to grow hay from spring until summer and then become pasture for sheep.

Further downriver there's the sudden sharp '*kraaaarrrkkk*!' of a grey heron as it takes off downwind. A skein of greylag geese flies over. Their plaintive drawn-out honking provides a counterpoint to the steady rhythmic beat of their wings. A straggler catches up and joins the 'v' formation just as its reflection glides across the clouds on the water's surface.

I cross a short wooden bridge to a narrower stretch of path opposite the long stretch of woodland I could see from the bridge. It's over half a mile long and set on a slope that comes right down to the river's edge. Ash and willow trees have self-seeded there. Some of the ashes are eighty feet tall. There are big willow trees too, but most are short, spread out along the bank with a few hawthorn bushes. If a tall tree falls across the river the authorities remove it, but otherwise the wood is left to itself. Trunks are festooned with ivy. There's lots of fallen timber, which is ideal for insects and fungi.

The river narrows at this point, and the morning sun is directly behind me. As I look across it's like peering into a cross section of a forest illuminated by theatrical lighting. It's perfect for watching the trees and wildlife on the far bank. Overhanging branches dip low towards the water and make ideal perches for kingfishers. There are none here today, but from what I've seen over the years this is where their family life could play out in the coming months. Hopefully there'll be courtship, fights over territory, nest building and the rearing of at least one brood of chicks.

The willows bring some early warmth and colour to the riverbank, the tips of their branches showing subtle shades of orange and pink. A pair of blue tits appears to be doing some early house-hunting in a tree hole, taking it in turns to dip in and out. Their feathers are brightening up for the mating season, and there's a real hint of blue in their plumage. A wren's whirring wings show a rufous tinge as it hurries from one side of the river to the other. I stand and watch for a while, then start to shiver. There's the sharp scent of impending snow as I turn round and walk back to the bridge. My shoulders are hunched as I hurry beneath moaning power lines, grateful to put the biting wind behind me, and head for home.

6 JANUARY: The wind has dropped and it's a lot warmer. It's a good day for a 'sound walk'. I'm a self-taught musician, and have made my living from music and sounds in many different ways, including making recordings of birdsong. I learnt to tell bird songs apart long before I knew what the songsters looked like. For me,

listening to natural sounds can be as nourishing as a good meal. I take them in, savour them, let them roll around in my head.

I walk downriver till I'm opposite the wood, then stop and close my eyes. A great tit is calling from the right, in a looping pattern that sounds like a bent wheel turning on a squeaky axle. Then, from high in the trees, a song thrush starts singing repetitive phrases: "*Did he do it? Did he? Did he?*" His song spins wildly down to the forest floor, as if he has a lot to say but fears no one is listening. Out of nowhere a Cetti's warbler makes me jump with a sudden loud '*whackwhackwhack!*' from the reeds at the water's edge. In complete contrast, a bullfinch starts to sing from deep in the trees with a breathless, creaky tone, like gentle air escaping from a bellows. The song's so tiny and undemonstrative that it could easily be missed altogether.

After a brief lull there's the drum roll of a great spotted woodpecker pecking at dead wood to attract a mate and mark his territory against other males. I walk slowly down the path towards it. The noise it makes is astonishingly loud and full, even though I'm listening from the other side of the river. I've tried hitting hollow trees and branches with sticks but never came close to matching that volume. And the speed of the roll is created by just one beak rather than the two drumsticks a human percussionist might use. What the bird so expertly does is to pick the most resonant parts of the tree and rap them repeatedly at just the right speed, between ten and sixteen times per second. Its beak isn't hitting the wood anything like as hard as it sounds to be. It's all in the technique. 🔊 1.1

From back near the bridge there's the distant tinny sound of someone using a road drill. For a while it sounds like the woodpecker might be listening to it and reacting with louder bursts of drumming. But then they both stop, and I walk on to Cotterstock lock and cross to the other side of the river.

When I meet the road, I turn left and pause at the millpond. It's roughly circular in shape, and water swirls into it as it comes under the bridge from the mill race. The main river is mostly slow and quiet but the water here is full of life and sound. Like the river in Kenneth Grahame's *The Wind in the Willows* it's: "gripping things with a gurgle and leaving them with a laugh".

I walk up from the old mill and pass through the village. At the start of the path that leads back towards home there's a mistle thrush singing. I can't see him, but he's high in an oak tree, a master musician pouring out beautiful, heartfelt repeats of simple two-chord phrases, with tension and resolution, like an in breath followed by an out breath. The tone has the fullness of a blackbird but there's a strangely moving edge to it.

I walk home with the sound playing in my ears and open the front door. Upstairs I can hear my wife Eleanor doing natural voice exercises in the light, airy room at the front. I go into my little music studio tucked away in an outhouse at the back, lean my harp against my shoulder and start to play. I'm trying to capture the essence of that sound, not to copy it exactly, but to feel the speed and the rhythm of it, the sense of space and the promise of spring. I find a recording of a mistle thrush made last summer and start it playing endlessly through loudspeakers on a loop. ◀ 1.2

Then I close my eyes and quietly and gently begin to improvise along with the sound. When I stop, I'm surprised to find I've been playing for nearly an hour.

I started my working life as a musical-instrument maker, which is one of the reasons I'm so intrigued by woodpeckers' use of natural materials to make such a glorious sound. I was making Celtic harps, lutes and guitars, and one day a friend who was a primary schoolteacher asked me to go into her school to talk about my work.

I found the children's interest and enthusiasm fascinating, and loved their creativity and the unfiltered way in which they looked at life. I ended up spending much of the next three decades visiting thousands of schools across the country, demonstrating stringed instruments from around the world and helping children make instruments from junk materials.

Along the way I visited Paraguay in South America and began to learn to play their remarkable version of the harp. After starting to compose and record music that was inspired by the river and woods around my home, it seemed natural to record local birdsong and work it into the overall sound. Then I began giving musical talks to adults and playing relaxation music in care homes for the elderly. So far it's been an unusual career in music, but a very interesting one.

7 JANUARY: The river is quiet in winter, and I don't meet many people on the path, but it's still prone to litter. Sometimes I spot the shiny colours of helium balloons that have landed in the bushes by the river. Often my eye is fooled into thinking I've seen a kingfisher when it's actually a blue or red fishing lure or scrap of coloured plastic hanging in a tree. The exact opposite happened today. I saw what looked like a shiny blue toffee paper caught up in the twigs on the far bank and just kept on walking. Until it moved and flew off.

I'm not seeing kingfishers back at the bridge now. They appear to have moved downstream as the river has slowed down and become less muddy. Backwaters tend to ice up when there's a hard frost, so they're better off where there's a steady flow. As the fishing gets easier, they'll naturally move back into other stretches of the river.

9 JANUARY: My foot slipped on the muddy path this morning. I didn't fall, but it tweaked a tendon in my ankle that's given trouble before. Luckily the pain soon wore off, but it reminded me of a period a few years ago when I walked for a long time with a slight limp. Despite that, I decided to do a trek of about fifty miles from Christchurch Harbour in Dorset to Stonehenge, following the line of the River Avon. It took four days, and I found the easiest way to walk was with my hands clasped across my stomach to balance the weight of my rucksack, while my right leg dragged slightly behind me on each step. For some reason it made me think of an older country parson doggedly limping his way down a church aisle to take a service, so I dubbed my new walking style 'parson's progress'.

Recalling that this morning got me thinking about Gilbert White, an eighteenth-century clergyman regarded as England's first naturalist. He spent most of his life in his home village of Selborne in Hampshire, and began systematically watching and recording wildlife locally at a time when most study was done on dead specimens in museums. He had a good ear for birdsong too. He was the first person to distinguish between similar types of warbler by their songs. He shared his discoveries in letters to friends and scientific colleagues with a warmth and directness that really brought the subject to life.

When I got home, I found a copy of White's *The Natural History Of Selborne* bought years ago in a second-hand bookshop. In a letter written in August 1778 he describes how birds can be identified by the different ways they fly and move: "The kestrel, or wind-hover, has a peculiar mode of hanging in the air in one place… owls move in a buoyant manner, as if lighter than air… herons seem incumbered with too much sail for their light bodies…" Then he writes: "The king-fisher darts along like an arrow". In one short sentence he conjures a perfect image of this bird's direct and rapid flight, which could be here and gone in less time than it takes to get the words out.

I once visited White's former home, which is now a museum. It looks out over a stretch of parkland that ends with a steep, beech-covered slope called the Hanger. This natural feature is three hundred feet high, and apart from being a striking and dramatic part of the landscape, it also focusses and amplifies the ambience of the trees and birdsong. Standing there, I could easily imagine some of the sounds he described at the time: "Brown wood-owls come down from the hanger in the dusk of the evening, and sit hooting all night on my wall-nut trees".

I walked the short distance to the village church where White used to take services. There's a stained-glass window in his memory that depicts St Francis preaching to the birds. All sixty of the species mentioned in White's writings are featured on it. There are a pair of kingfishers amongst them, set in a corner with the glowing colours beautifully brought out by the light coming through the glass into the darkened church.

Back in White's garden I came across a reconstruction of his personal design for a bird hide. He called it a "wine-pipe". It looked delightfully eccentric, almost sculptural, and was fashioned from a large upright port barrel fitted with a thatched roof. Part of the barrel was cut away and there was a seat fixed inside with just enough room for one person to sit in it facing outwards. The base was mounted on a bearing so it could rotate round through 360 degrees. He'd sit there with netting stretched across the opening and watch birds without disturbing them. I sat in it and swivelled it gently round with my feet like a child on a playground roundabout. It was one of many lovely moments in a fascinating day out.

10 JANUARY: Bob gets in touch. He lives locally and we know of each other but haven't met. He's never seen a kingfisher, and could I help? He's seen some of my photos and knows that I take them along the river. Where are the best places to see one?

I invite him to join me on a walk, saying that nothing in nature is guaranteed, but at least if we don't spot one I can suggest where to look in future. We meet at the bridge and I point out the two perches next to it, though today they're empty.

We set off downstream along the riverbank. As we walk, I explain that if we're lucky a kingfisher will fly by. That's how most people will see one at first. If the light is dim you may just make out a dark profile flying fast and straight and close to the river's surface. But if the sun's bright and shining at the right angle there's a chance you may be treated to that unforgettable bright blue flash of its back feathers.

Kingfishers are solitary except during the breeding season. They need big territories to find enough fish to eat. The territories are usually lengths of rivers, lakes or streams up to two miles long, though kingfishers can also live in saltwater estuaries. They guard them from others so the birds are spread out and can be hard to spot. It's difficult to see them perching, though it helps if you notice one flying and see where it lands. They like to settle on a thin bare branch a few feet above the water where they can get a good view of the fish. They may also perch on posts and jetties close to the water's edge, which can be dotted with the telltale splashes of their white droppings.

If it's not too far away, you may be able to make out a kingfisher by its long-billed silhouette. But it's unlikely that you'll see the whole shape of the bird to begin with. Instead, you're looking for a few pixels of colour among the trees or shrubs at the water's edge. If you search carefully enough a tiny patch of blue or orange breast feathers may jump out at you. Sometimes they may be reflected in the water below where the bird is perching. You need patience and sharp eyes.

Kingfishers also make a whistling '*tzee*' sound which can be enormously helpful in finding them. ◀ 1.3 At certain times of the year I nearly always hear one before I see it. The calls resemble a high-pitched dog whistle. I sometimes think I'm listening to a kingfisher when it's actually a few quick blasts from a dog owner further down the bank.

We get almost to the side weir without seeing one but meet other people who tell us they already have. Then I hear a call and see a familiar profile shoot downstream. We walk across the weir, and I can see where it's landed, perched against a patch of sunlit ivy on the far bank. I point it out, but at first Bob can't spot it. That's not surprising if you're not used to looking for small birds against a tangled background. But then a passing walker stops and lends him a pair of binoculars, and he ends up with a fantastic close-up view. The bird stays put for a few moments before taking off across the meadows. Bob's beaming as we set off back towards Oundle. So am I. It's always a joy to see a kingfisher, but a double joy to share it with someone else.

12 JANUARY: I realised a long time ago that a hole appears around you as you walk in nature. If you stop and sit for twenty minutes and move nothing but your eyes, it will fill in again, and you'll see and hear all sorts of things. I'd thought that was because birds and animals were naturally wary of a moving human, and only gradually went back to what they were doing before. Then I realised that it's me who changes too. If I sit still and observe for twenty minutes the breathing slows, the body disappears. Things come and go without undue physical or mental reactions. It's a form of meditation that opens you out to the world.

This morning I cross the river at Cotterstock lock and sit motionless on the wall by the millpond for forty minutes or more. There is the soft sound of falling water, and rooks caw from the trees towards the church. A song thrush sings from the thicket on the right. Small fry start jumping out of the water in rows like flying fish, and a long streak of green and white belly flashes close to the surface. It's a pike, a large one, getting on for three feet long.

I stand up and walk on through the village, then turn left onto the path to return home through the wood. At the edge of Snipe Meadow a kestrel is perched at head height on an exposed branch, looking directly into the hazy morning sun. I walk a few steps towards it, then stop. Then a few more steps, slower this time. It doesn't move. The bird seems to be either dazzled or dozing. I take in the dark and orange-brown chequerboard pattern of its overlapping feathers, its large eye and the downward curve of its beak. The sun's warmth teases thin trails of steam from the rushes behind it. Otherwise, time stands still. Then it appears to wake up and see me. It takes off from the branch, then hovers low for a few seconds before wheeling across the meadow and dipping down beyond the far side of the river.

16 JANUARY: By the middle of January it's noticeably brighter, and the sun's higher in the sky. The day's length has increased by twenty minutes since the start of the year. It'll be forty minutes longer still by the end of the month. The gradual accumulation of light and warmth is crucial to kingfishers. It brings more time each day to look for fish and brighter light by which to see them. The fish themselves become far more active. In cold water their systems slow, and they stay deeper. As the water warms up they move about and eat more. They're an easier target.

There's also less chance of the river icing over. That's a major threat to kingfishers as it stops them diving into the water to catch fish. In countries with predictable freezing winters kingfishers tend to migrate south or fly to saltwater coasts. But in the UK the winter months are generally mild so they stay put. An unusually harsh year can be disastrous for them. In the mid-1930s the Oxford Ornithological Society organised a survey covering sixty miles of the River Thames. They found over thirty kingfisher nests. After an exceptionally frosty winter in 1939 they surveyed the same stretch during the following spring and summer, and found only two nests. Luckily kingfishers can have as many as three broods of up to six chicks each year. Numbers on the Thames bounced back fairly quickly.

In the long, hard winter of 1963 it's estimated that up to eighty-five per cent of kingfishers perished in the UK. In many areas they were almost eliminated. Normally they would have flown south or west to the coast looking for water that was free of ice. But in that year even the sea froze. Again the numbers recovered, but the mortality figures make heart-stopping reading.

20 JANUARY: About halfway along the wood there's a short concrete bridge over a weir. Here a stream leaves the river and flows round the back of Cotterstock lock. A few years ago I had an encounter there with an otter. I spotted something grey-brown under the branches on the far bank, which quickly disappeared. Then a nose and tail emerged in the middle of the river and made an effortless, graceful dive with the tail sliding up then slipping below the water.

It was windy and the river was choppy, so I couldn't see the stream of bubbles that would normally show where it might come up next. I was busy looking back and forth when a head popped out. It was directly below and in front of me, just six feet away. It's unnatural to stay cool in such a close encounter with a wild animal, so I shouted with surprise and nearly fell over backwards. I managed a glimpse of its whiskered face disappearing back underwater, all the while looking straight at me, then there was a muffled 'ploomp' from its tail and the animal was gone.

I was shaking and had to sit on a stile for a few minutes. The experience had been wonderful but disturbing. It wasn't just that it was so close, but I'd seen in the otter the face of my late father. The dark eyes and whiskers coming up towards the surface were so familiar. Dad was a strong swimmer with a big, bristly RAF moustache, and he used to swim underwater then emerge suddenly at the edge of the swimming pool to give us a scare. He was a complex and troubled man who didn't take well to the responsibilities of fatherhood. I never really knew where I was with him. I thought about that episode with the otter for a long time, and what it might mean. It was as if nature was telling me something. I'm not sure I have any answers even now, but what I do know is that I've never seen an otter there since.

24 JANUARY: There's a glorious sunrise from the back door this morning as bright corrugated streaks of red and yellow light up the eastern sky. The patterns change as I watch. It's a genuine shepherd's warning because the forecast is for heavy snow. It arrives around midday. The garden becomes a whirling snow dome of giant flakes that settle fast. After a couple of hours there's a covering of four inches. As soon as it stops, I dress up warm and head for the river.

Fresh snow changes the look of a landscape. It softens sharp edges, blurs contrasts, and reduces colours to varieties of white light. It affects sounds too. There's a hush that seems to shrink the world and hem you in. Echoes are blunted and volumes flattened out. It's not clear where sounds or voices are coming from. As I walk across the bridge the traffic on the bypass is so quiet that it's either stopped altogether or is moving at a crawl.

I'm listening to my own footsteps treading in the snow and wondering how to describe what I'm hearing. John Clare, the nineteenth-century Romantic poet, was born and brought up just fifteen miles away from here, in the village of Helpston. He included a lot of sounds in his poetry and used the Northamptonshire dialect word "crumping" to describe the tramp of feet in fresh snow. That's the perfect word for what I'm hearing right now.

When I get to the river, I'm hoping to find wild animal tracks in the virgin snow, but others have got there before me. Once a few dogs and people have walked a path the marks get confused. After a heavy snowfall a few years ago, however, I was the first human to walk right along the river. To start with, I could see plenty of tracks from waterbirds and rabbits, but then I began picking up a set of dog-like prints that were likely to be a fox.

The marks were very neat and careful, and I had followed them for a while before noticing something puzzling. This wasn't the normal pattern of a dog's tracks with four separate prints marking the succession of front and back paws. It looked like the fox was walking on two legs like a human. Foxes are known to play fight on their hind legs, but they don't stay upright for long. I eventually worked out what was happening. It was placing a front paw down, then as it was lifting it and reached forward it placed the back paw on the same side in the same track.

This approach must make moving silently much easier, because it can see where each front paw is going and be sure the back paws will always land in the same place. It could be a warmer and easier way of walking in snow too. With tracks that ape a human's walk it's easy to see how so many legends and stories of wily foxes might arise.

25 JANUARY: The snow's still here this morning. When I open the back door at 7am the world's hushed. There's barely a whisper from the bypass. A single robin's singing its sad winter song from a snow-laden shrub in the garden. 🔊 1.4

Later, I go out to try and get a seasonal photo of a kingfisher. I stay out by the river for a long time but there's no sign of one. The combination of bad weather and murky water makes it difficult for them to see beneath the surface and catch fish. I'm starting to get really concerned. In the end I give up thinking about photographs and just pray to see one alive. The prayer's finally granted as I walk opposite the wood. There's a call, and a kingfisher flies past and settles on a branch. I can see its profile as it peers down. Green ivy leaves frame its brightly coloured feathers, and there's snow on the slope behind it.

I get the camera out and click away until the bird flies off. Then I look at the screen to sort through all those great shots. But no pictures appear, just the words: 'no memory card'. I forgot to put the card in the camera. It's sitting uselessly back home connected to the laptop. That's not the first time that's happened. Hopefully it'll be the last, at least for a while. Despite that, it's been a great walk. I've seen and heard a kingfisher thriving despite the floods and bad weather. And anyway, the best pictures are always the ones that got away, the ones inside your own head.

28 JANUARY: There's a snowmelt mist on the meadows as I look down from the bridge. It's raining hard and the path's going to be difficult. I decide to walk to Barnwell Country Park instead. The river takes a long, slow bend as it winds upstream around Oundle towards the park. It would take over an hour to get there along the riverbank, but only fifteen minutes to walk the pavements through town. I decide to take the easier option.

The park includes flooded gravel pits that attract a lot of waterbirds. There are pools with overhanging branches and reed beds that are ideal for kingfishers. When I arrive I'm delighted to see a flock of a few hundred lapwings settled in a field nearby. I love their shape, their mewling call, and the way the wings of a flock show black, then white, then black again as they turn against the sky. A small group huddle together, their upticked head feathers looking like plumes on the caps of Tsarist officers. Then they take off in an untidy lolloping flap, half-circling to gain height against a darkening grey sky before twinkling off downwind towards the east.

A few years ago I watched a lapwing murmuration over a flooded field by the river. They gathered and pulsed like an alien entity above the dry raised fields to the south. Then they poured into the space above the floods, diving towards the water and rising again as wigeon ducks whistled in alarm. The wings of the outer birds struck the water as the whole flock turned, throwing up splashes of spray from the surface. They sailed over the top of me, two groups racing across each other in a blizzard of loud cries and fluttering wings. Then just as quickly they flew back across the fields, and it was quiet again.

29 JANUARY: I usually wear walking boots, but after the recent rain sections of the path are under a few inches of water. I set out with my wellingtons on. I'm bowling along thinking about sounds and the way they change with the seasons. Leafless willows sound lower and darker in the wind, like distant surf. Birdsong appears louder and brighter as it echoes through the empty trees. And my boots are making satisfying squelches in the mud.

On the way back from Cotterstock I get to a bridge over a brook that flows towards the river from Glapthorn. It's burst its banks and flooded right across the fields and path. The water's muddy, quick-flowing and knee-deep. Even with wellingtons there's a risk of overtopping. The sensible thing is to go back the way I came, but I don't fancy that. So I weave through the undergrowth into the wood and find a tree that's fallen across the stream. Then I edge along its slippery trunk, sideways on, clinging to the few remaining branches to stay upright. A few minutes later I arrive safely on the other side with a few scratches and a priceless feeling of connection with the nine-year-old me who first learned outdoor life skills on daily adventures in the woods.

I carry on along the path and come to a large puddle. It has an old railway sleeper lying across it as a makeshift bridge. There's some water on top of it but that's OK. I've got my boots on. Except that when I step on the bridge it's not fixed, it's floating. One boot goes right down into the water and fills up, and it still hasn't reached the bottom. The other fills as I flail about trying to keep my balance. Thank goodness for a nearby branch, which stops me from sprawling.

Safely back on dry land I empty out each boot, giggling. Plenty of whiffy water pours out, but disappointingly, no fish. I wring out my socks and put my boots back on. They make cold squishy sounds for the rest of the walk which don't stop when I reach the tarmac. It's been good fun though, no harm done. And at least I won't have to own up to my mum when I get home.

30 JANUARY: The snowmelt floods are still pouring downstream from the Northamptonshire catchment. I barely make it through the floods again this morning, but it turns out to be worth it. I watch a female kingfisher for about twenty minutes. She spends a few minutes at a time on different perches, some low down near the water's surface and some higher up in a tree. Sometimes she faces away from the river itself, looking down into the flooded puddles where the path would normally be. It could be that fish are swimming there in the shallower waters. Even so, she only dives twice in the time that I'm watching and doesn't catch anything. As I walk back through the woods the staring eyes of a sparrowhawk

whizz past at head height as it weaves an effortless high-speed slalom through the trees.

31 JANUARY: I've left the house at about the same time each day for a month and walked across the bridge and down the far side of the river from Oundle to Cotterstock. Then I've come back along the near side whenever I could. What have I learned?

The whole extent of the walk can be seen from the bridge at the start, and sometimes when the rain stops and the sun comes out, a rainbow arches over the whole scene.

The rough meadow on the left side of the river contrasts with the grazed area on the right. Both flood, but the right drains quicker.

Birdsong has swelled from just rooks, robins and great tits at the start of the month to a hint of spring at the end. There have been song thrushes and mistle thrushes, woodpeckers, buzzards, ravens, skylarks and the weird cry of lapwings flying high overhead.

Grey herons will eat all kinds of things. I've watched with appalled fascination as one caught and swallowed a large mole in one gulp. I've walked on a hard-frozen path that only the next day was a slippery mud bath. I've marvelled at how well the wood shelters the river path from a northwest wind, even when the branches are roaring so loud you can't hear the water rushing over the weir. I started counting the rings on the stump of a dead tree that fell across the river, then got close to my own age and stopped because I began to feel superstitious.

And through it all I've seen kingfishers flying and fishing and perching, heard their high calls, and caught the sun's flash off their feathers as they sped past the trees and followed the bend to the next part of the river.

FEBRUARY

1 FEBRUARY: The nature writer and artist Denys Watkins-Pitchford was born in Lamport in Northamptonshire in 1905. After a childhood spent exploring the local countryside he studied art. Later he worked as an art teacher, but also wrote and illustrated many books about nature under the pen name 'BB'. They included *The Little Grey Men*, which won the Carnegie Medal for children's books. In 1964 he moved to Sudborough, which is less than ten miles from Oundle. Two years later he hired a boat and explored the local river. He wrote a very enjoyable book about it called *A Summer on the Nene*.

Today I'm standing by the weir downstream from the bridge. I'm looking across the river to the wood on the far bank and wondering how it will look and feel in the months to come. BB describes in his book how he tied up the boat very close to where I'm standing now. It was a hot day in May, and he was glad of the shade under the willows. The meadows shimmered, and "larks carolled" overhead. The song of blackcaps and whitethroats echoed in the trees "like fairy bells." Today all I can see and hear is cold bare trees and a few chirps from a blue tit.

In 2008, at the beginning of each month, I took a fifteen-second video clip of the view across the river from this spot. The idea was to combine them all into a three-minute film showing the riverbank as it changed through the seasons. I thought the finished result would mostly be a botanical record of a magnificent ash tree on the far bank that has a long horizontal branch that juts out at right angles from its lower trunk. It would show the changes of shape and colour as the leaves budded and fell through the year.

I hadn't thought about the wildlife and the people passing along the river in front of the tree and on the slope behind it. The finished film ended up being much more interesting. There were dog walkers trudging in a March blizzard, and in April a scrap-festooned narrowboat passed through looking like something out of a *Mad Max* movie. In other months there were an aggressive swan, the streak of an all-but-invisible kingfisher, broken branches borne along by late-summer floods and the hypnotic swirl of falling autumn leaves. The soundtrack featured cuckoos, robins, red kites, water rushing over the weir, the splash of paddles and the slow beat of a diesel engine.

Sounds have been important throughout my life, though I might not have realised it at the time. I remember being taken to a parade as a toddler and hearing the different instruments of a band as they marched past. There were the trumpets and clarinets, and the jolting beat of the big bass drum.

As my dad was in the military we lived in many places in England and abroad. In Hong Kong we went to a circus with jaunty music. Then there was the gently musical street call, rising to a yodel on the last note, of a Chinese man who used to ride a bicycle up the hill to our flats and ladle a sweet rice drink out of a container on the back.

When we came back to England I often stayed with my nan in Bournemouth. The wind off the sea made a reassuring sound at the bedroom window while I was tucked up at night. Later, near an airbase in rural Hampshire, I was allowed to walk on my own down a country lane to junior school for the first time. I stopped to look at some bright blue forget-me-nots and a telephone wire overhead started humming in the wind. I was scared and fascinated at the same time.

We spent a couple of years living in Norway, and there was the swish of skis in winter, and the sound of a waterfall on the far side of a fjord during a summer trip to the north. When we moved back to Sussex there was the crunch of shingle underfoot on the beach at Climping, and I'd ride my bike through the green lanes and hear the roar of cars hurtling round the racing circuit at Goodwood.

Much later I sat in an oak-panelled study, panicked and unable to concentrate during a mind-numbing philosophy tutorial. A blackbird started singing outside the window and brought me some calm. More decades passed, and a long period of anxiety began to lift after I stopped on a desperate winter evening's walk to listen to dry beech leaves rustling in the wind. It was the first time I'd noticed anything outside of the swirl of my mind and emotions for months, and it was a turning point. I came away with the conviction that everything I needed to thrive, and everything I needed to learn about the world, was within walking distance of my own front door. After that I walked near the river and through woods and forests every day that I could. And I made sure that I never stopped looking and listening.

2 FEBRUARY: There was a grey heron in a tree by Snipe Meadow this morning. Usually I see them standing at the river's edge or out in the fields, waiting for fish or frogs, or even rats and moles. I think of them as secret policemen in their grey coats, watching and hiding in plain sight. When the moment comes their necks gradually start to descend towards their prey. Then there's a sudden curve back of the head and an explosive strike with that fearsome sharp beak. Then the head tilts back again as the prey slides down that long, thin throat.

3 FEBRUARY: As I stand on the bridge a kingfisher flashes under the arches and zips smoothly down the middle of the river before banking round the bend to the left and out of sight. Then a cormorant flaps back the other way and lands with a splash before diving underwater and emerging with a fish.

I often see groups of up to six cormorants perched in the tall ash trees downstream. They're large birds, and their beaks and eyes and dark plumage can make them appear cruel and forbidding. But the light sometimes brings out subtle shadings and patterns in their feathers. They look their best when standing with wings stretched out to the sides to catch the warmth of the sun. In medieval heraldry this was thought to resemble the sign of the cross, and they became symbols of nobility.

While I'm thinking about this the clock strikes at St Peter's church, and I look back towards the spire which dominates Oundle. At two hundred feet tall it's the highest in a county that's famous for them. It reminds me of a true story connecting the church and the river from the middle of the seventeenth century when the town was a Puritan stronghold. I decide to walk back into town to look at an eagle lectern that was at the centre of it.

I leave the bridge behind and pass green sports pitches on my left and modern houses on the right, then carry on towards North Street. The town's set back from the river on higher ground, and it and the surrounding countryside are part of a low ridge of hills that runs from the Cotswolds right up into Lincolnshire. Beneath that there's a limestone bedrock that was formed under the sea during the Jurassic period. Limestone from local quarries was used to build many of the elegant buildings in the town's historic centre.

By now I'm walking into the old part of town. The narrow road is flanked by stone-built period houses which are mostly joined up in terraces. There's a wide range of heights and styles, and a higgledy-piggledy roofline tiled with Collyweston slate. There was once a big brewery nearby, and many of the buildings used to be pubs. A cottage industry of lacemakers lived and worked in some of the smaller houses.

I cross the road and climb the steps to the churchyard, glad to leave the traffic behind. My footsteps ring on the flagstone path as I pass by yew trees and well-kept graves dotted with snowdrops. On the far side, groups of students from Oundle School carry books and call out to each other as they walk between classes.

I glance up at the clock and the spire looming overhead. I'm checking to see if the peregrine falcon which occasionally visits is perched on a stone carving near the top. It's not there, so I pass through the open blue outer doors and down the well-worn steps into church. It's remarkably warm and welcoming, and seems lighter inside than out. Hundreds of light wooden chairs are arranged looking towards the altar. On the right there's a tall, polished brass lectern shaped like an eagle with outstretched wings. It has a large open Bible resting on it and is fixed to a stand. The eagle's beak is at eye level, and the stand widens as it descends to a base with brass claws that rest on the floor. I try to push it sideways but it won't budge. It's very heavy.

During the English Civil War a group of Cromwell's men decided the eagle symbol was idolatrous. They stormed into the church, dragged the lectern to the river, and threw it in. No one knows exactly where, but it could have been down by the bridge. It stayed buried in the mud for two centuries before being rediscovered when the main channel was dredged. Still intact, it was cleaned up and restored to the church, where it's still in regular use today.

While I'm looking at it there's a sound behind me. I hadn't noticed a lady quietly arranging flowers near the font. I think of the generations of people who've built and cared for this place, and the thoughts of those who were upset when the lectern was taken. It would have needed hard and patient work to bring it back to its rightful place and clean off the blue-green verdigris. People still polish it today in one of the regular small acts of service and devotion that connect past with present. As I leave the church I picture a cormorant high above the meadows on a branch downstream, wings stretched out like a cross against a bright blue sky.

4 FEBRUARY: This morning I decided not to go out in the heavy rain but to spend a whole day in my studio working on some music. At the end of last year I started collaborating on the internet with Fara Afifi, a musician I've never met but who shares a love of birds and birdsong. We were originally put in touch by a BBC radio producer after we appeared separately on the same programme to talk about how birds inspire our music. I later composed a piece

on the harp to go with a video I'd made of a starling murmuration. Fara offered to write and play some string arrangements for it.

She recorded some wonderfully atmospheric voice tracks too, which we're turning into a song. I watch the video again and try to think myself back to a windy lakeside in a freezing November dusk, gazing up at the shifting shapes against a colour-wash sunset. I start to sketch out some ideas for lyrics: *wings beating, hearts racing, criss-crossing, merging / swaying and turning, and tumbling down / billowing ribbons write words in the heavens / waves crash on hilltops, the lake fills with sound…*

I spend the rest of the day adding a guitar part and trying to work the sound of my handpan into the mix. This is a modern tuned percussion instrument that looks like a burnished-metal flying saucer. When played with the fingertips it makes a lovely ethereal sound, and the first results are promising. I mix down some rough versions of the track and send them by email for Fara to listen to. It's been a good day's work.

5 FEBRUARY: The air's full of birdsong. There are a few notes from a blackbird by the bridge, the first I've heard this year. I can hear a mistle thrush singing near the old railway station. Great tits and song thrushes are spinning out their calls in the early spring light. There's the downward rush of a chaffinch, and a skylark singing by the path on the way back from Cotterstock.

As I walk back by the river I hear a kingfisher before I see it. There's a flurry of piercing calls as it passes and lands on a branch just feet away. I can see its profile peering down at the water. It hasn't noticed me. I stay as still as possible, taking in its electric-blue feathers and the neat white patches at its neck. It holds the same pose for a few moments, then there's a single explosive '*tzee!*' and it takes off to fish elsewhere. The thin branch it was perched on sways gently back and forth.

One of the reasons that kingfishers are so hard to spot is that sitting still while waiting for prey is an important part of their fishing technique. Even when a branch is being blown about by the wind, they can hold their heads perfectly steady as they focus on their target. Then they suddenly plunge into the water in a surprise attack. They don't pursue prey underwater like a cormorant. Instead they rely on getting the angles just right so they can grab the fish immediately and head straight back to a perch with it.

Kingfishers' extraordinary eyesight allows them to see below the surface before they dive and to make allowances for the sun's glare and the bending effect of light when it travels through water. Like much larger birds of prey, including eagles and owls, they have twice as many photoreceptors in each eye as humans do. Their eyes also contain special oils that are thought to improve colour perception.

These adaptations make kingfishers very aware of movements, including those of anyone walking nearby. They will usually take off before a human gets close. I was lucky that this one chose to land slightly forward of me and instantly became focussed on the water beneath.

6 FEBRUARY: I've walked by the river almost every day this year. It's time for a change. I drive a few miles up the valley past Southwick to walk along the edge of some woods which are a remnant of Rockingham Forest, a royal hunting ground dating from the time of William the Conqueror. There are a few very old oak trees dotted

about, but it's managed by the Forestry Commission so there are a variety of trees and habitats. Some are suitable for nightingales. In April I'll be up there again to listen for them.

Where I usually walk by the river there's the distant hum of the A605 and the sound of floods going over a weir. As I get out of the car here the first impression is totally different. Just natural sounds set against silence. There's a greater sense of space and clarity, more definition to the harsh kronking calls of a pair of ravens as they fly across the ploughed fields. ◀) 2.5

I walk up a steep concrete road and step carefully over the cattle grid by Crossway Hand Farm. The stone farm buildings feel isolated, almost fortified. By the entrance there's a tall dead oak, stripped of its bark. Its bare branches twist like flames into the sky. Nearby there's a strange sculptural sign featuring an uplifted metal hand with fingers that are welded from steel piping. A fox trots across the track as I ramble along the edge of the trees. It's starting to show the full rich red of its spring coat.

Near Boar's Head Farm there's a pond. It usually has a realistic, life-sized ornamental crocodile lurking in the shallows. It made me jump the first time I walked by at dusk to listen to nightingales. Whether it's been covered by floodwater or stored away for the winter, I'm disconcerted that it's gone. It's as if it might have waddled away of its own accord and be waiting behind a tree trunk.

I follow the path through a thin stand of trees then walk out into sloping fields. There's a territorial battle going on between half a dozen skylarks over an area the size of a football pitch. Normally you hear them when they're a speck overhead, as hard to pick out as John Clare's "dust spot in the sunny skies". Then they have a gentle trilling quality that W.H. Hudson, a nature writer of the late nineteenth and early twentieth centuries, called "sunshine translated into sound". ◀ 2.6 It's the sort of ambience that Vaughan Williams captures so well in *The Lark Ascending*. But these larks are hovering, low over the fields, occasionally darting at one another to assert their territory. They sound jagged, spontaneous and loud. More free jazz than classical.

I walk back down towards the edge of the forest and the skylarks' song fades till I can barely hear it. Alongside the path there's a dilapidated wire fence. The top strand is the thickness of a washing line. It's loose, but not too loose. I can't resist twanging it. It gives a lovely low scuttering sound, like a distant helicopter. I can hear the wave passing on from one fence post to the next through the open hasps that have been used to fix it. When it gets to the post at the far end the sound wave starts to make its way back again before petering out.

On the other side of the fence there's a stream. As I walk alongside it there are low gurgles and swishes as the water runs past. In places it's hidden by brambles, and becomes muffled and distant. Elsewhere, lumps of rock that were lifted during ploughing have been dumped in the stream's bed. They create small pools behind them, and the water bubbles as it escapes around their hard edges. In drought years this type of stream often dries up, and my ears have cried out for these sounds in the landscape. Now they're everywhere.

During geography lessons at school I remember studying watersheds and the catchment areas of rivers. I couldn't see the point at the time, but now I can picture all the rainfall in this area making its way down towards the river. This stream drains towards the river at Perio Mill. Ditches and streams on the other side of the hill join the Willow Brook and flow into the main river downstream of Fotheringhay.

I imagine all the different sounds of the water that makes its way into the Nene from all its sources and drains towards the sea. The patter of rain, and drips from frosted branches in the morning sun. The gushing springs, weirs and sluices. And the rhythmic pull of the tides as the river flows into the estuary at the Wash.

7 FEBRUARY: I'm back by the river again, and as usual my eyes and ears are scanning for sights and sounds that stand out. There's a grey-brown shape on a post some way in the distance. I'm beginning to think it might be an owl, but I've never seen one there in the light before. I'm getting closer and there's something not quite right about it. There's no movement, and it's a bit squat and low.

I'm closer now, and I can see it's a flat cap. Then as I reach it the penny finally drops. It's one of mine. In fact, it's quite a stylish tweed one that Eleanor gave me for Christmas. I'm not sure how it left my head and got forgotten, but it must have lain in the grass for a week or two and then been hung up by someone so it could be seen.

It's none the worse for wear, and smells washing-line fresh with a hint of creosote. When I put it on it feels slightly tighter, so it may have shrunk a little in the rain. That's no bad thing. It's prone to fly off my head if a big lorry goes by when I'm walking across the bridge.

I straighten it up and carry on walking: "*the man who mistook his hat for an owl*".

8 FEBRUARY: There was an inch or two of snow overnight, and it's so calm that it's settled on the thinnest of the twigs and branches.

My frozen breath hangs in the air as I walk the wooded path back along the river from Cotterstock. The wood's full of black and white contrasts. The reflected light seems almost blue. Suddenly a pair of kingfishers whizzes straight along the path towards me. They're flying together, and one veers past my left ear at the last moment. It's so close I can hear the rapid whirr of wings. The other turns on its tail just before it gets to me and flies to a perch about fifty feet away. I have time to take one quick photo and it's gone again.

I look at the image on my camera. I can just make out the orange lower beak of a female. She's perched on a willow, and her bright feathers look extraordinarily exotic against the tangled lattice of snowy-white branches. There are patches of dark bark on the twig below her feet where she scattered the snow as she landed.

I try to process what I've seen and heard, and realise I've taken in much more than I would have a month ago. Practice has speeded up my focus and retention. At one time I'd have been too startled to register what I was experiencing. Now there's time to think. I'd noticed that the kingfishers had been calling as they flew towards me. There was a sound quality I'd not heard before. It was quiet, more of a warble or twitter than a series of whistles or pips. The male (assuming it was a male) carried on making the sound as he flew close by.

It's not always easy to tell whether behaviour between two birds constitutes aggression or courtship, but I think the sounds they were making would have been much louder if they were rivals. It's the first time this year that I've seen two kingfishers together. It looks like the mating season might have started.

When I get home, I look in a 1969 book called *The Kingfisher* by Rosemary Eastman. It was a follow-up to a remarkably successful film, *The Private Life of the Kingfisher*, which she made with her husband Ronald. It was the first wildlife film shown in colour on BBC television and was part of a revolution in the way nature was portrayed on screen.

The Eastmans, then a young couple in their twenties, spent a lot of time watching and filming kingfishers on the River Test near their home in Whitchurch, Hampshire. Ronald worked part-time as a cinema projectionist while they gradually got better equipment and worked out ways of coaxing kingfishers closer to their homemade hides. They even managed to film inside the nests themselves. Many of the behaviours they saw were captured on film for the first time.

Their approach was inspired by a German film, *The Woodpeckers of the Black Forest*, made in 1955 by Heinz Seilmann. Naturalist and wildlife artist Peter Scott saw it at a conference in Switzerland and brought it back to England. Scott convinced the BBC to show the film on its *Look* programme, and it was a huge hit with the public. It started a trend of films showing the intimate lives of animals and birds that, a decade later, resulted in the BBC collaborating with the Eastmans to create a colour film about kingfishers. Scott narrated the programme.

In her book Eastman recalls seeing pairs of kingfishers chasing and calling wildly from late December onwards. By 13 February they were already fishing together and calling softly. I think it's highly likely that the birds I saw were a pair. Their courtship could already be well advanced.

9 FEBRUARY: As I came through the wood this morning a robin came quietly down through the branches to check me out.

It perched about eight feet away and we watched each other for several minutes. Of all wild birds the robin is the one you can most easily share a moment with. There's no knowing exactly what's going on in their heads, but they're confident and curious enough to sit close by and watch you without flinching. The relationship is most obviously beneficial to them where food is involved. For a robin, a person digging in the garden and bringing up worms harks right back to them watching animals that dig the earth like moles, wild boars and badgers.

There's a lovely song dating from the early sixteenth century called *Ah, Robin*. It was written by William Cornysh and appears in a collection of music that may have been performed at the royal court, known as *Henry VIII's Book*. The poet is thinking about his 'leman', an early English word for sweetheart, and addresses his thoughts to a robin:

> *Ah, Robin, gentle Robin,*
> *Tell me how thy leman doth*
> *and thou shalt know of mine.*

The tune has the melancholy feel of a robin's song, and there's a real sense that Cornysh is talking about an actual bird rather than using it as a poetic symbol.

The robin I'm watching is still perched close by. Whether it's waiting for me to provide food in some way I don't know. It certainly seems very relaxed. Eventually I turn away and walk back along the path. Its thin ribbon of winter song reels out through the trees behind me like the curlicue pen strokes of an ornate Tudor signature.

10 FEBRUARY: For the last two days I've seen a kingfisher in the same tree just downstream of Snipe Meadow. It's there again this morning, and I'm trying to get a photo of it. Photographing birds sounds like a romantic thing to do, and sometimes it is. But today there are so many twigs in the way that I'm down on my knees in the mud and slush trying to get a good angle. I would have stretched out on my stomach if necessary. People I see regularly on my walks have become used to my wild-eyed and dishevelled figure. I'd expect strangers to give me a wide berth. But when people see my camera, it's always a good conversation opener. Without it my social life would be much less interesting.

A couple come walking along the path. They look relaxed and smiley, enjoying the outdoors. Both wear walking boots. He has a trim grey beard, and she's wearing a colourful red jacket and hat. They ask if I've seen anything interesting. I tell them about the kingfisher that's just flown off. They say they've never seen one here by the river, but often saw one by their garden pond when they lived down south. They'd spot it from the conservatory, sitting in a shrub next to the water. They smile, and their eyes go distant at the memory of it.

In his 1982 book *The Kingfisher*, David Boag quotes an elderly lady telling him: "only the righteous ever see the kingfisher". That's obviously debatable, but it gives a sense of how special an encounter can be. It's as if the observer has been chosen or blessed in some way, and people fully appreciate that.

We wish each other luck, and a good day, and they walk on down the path. There are lots of birds in flocks as I walk back through the meadows: lapwings, fieldfares, redwings and pied wagtails. Standing in the shallows by the bridge is a single great egret, a snow-white heron. Its ghostly silhouette shines against the dark honey backdrop of the tall stone arches.

11 FEBRUARY: There's a bitter east wind this morning. The first part of the river is very exposed and chilly. Even wearing two woolly hats and multiple scarves doesn't make much difference. It's not all bad though. The mud has frozen and in places that makes walking easier. The river level's nearly back to normal after the latest bout of flooding.

Birds seem to conserve their energy in this weather and there's very little song. It's as if it's not worth their while competing with the roar of the wind in the trees, which is hugely impressive. There's a lone willow just past the bridge. I think of it as my portal to another world of sound. Today its branches speak of deep, pounding surf crashing continuously on a long, sloping beach. On the far side of the river, below Snipe Meadow, skeletal trees creak and shudder with each bone-chilling gust. Impatient waves lap against the driftwood that's been trapped under the branches near the bank.

I watch a swan take off into the wind, making little headway despite its powerful wings. It slowly rises above the reeds, then banks straight away downwind towards the west. A grey wagtail forages by a frozen weir, darting among the icicles dangling from a thorny broken branch. The freeze has stilled the sound of rushing water, but there are shrill whistles as the wind tears through a rough wooden fence nearby.

12 FEBRUARY: It's a fine, calm day and the wind's dropped. I take some recording gear with me to try and capture some birdsong in the woods by the river. I use a digital recorder and a

pair of small microphones that are designed for public speakers to wear on their lapels. They work very well for natural sounds. I move through the woods, listening for a pleasing combination of different songs and calls. The best spot is right by the river. Each microphone has a bulldog clip on it. I fasten them to some ivy on a tree, about as far apart from each other as the distance between my own ears. I start the recorder and wait in silence.

After a while a woodpecker starts tapping out gentle rhythmic patterns from a branch overhead, like a tentative knock on a door. It's not making the full drumming sound, though there's some of that from another woodpecker further off. These are quiet, probing taps made while looking for grubs and insects. Normally they come from much higher in the trees and are difficult to hear clearly. But this bird is so close that I deliberately don't look up in case I disturb it. After a few minutes it stops, and I switch off the recorder.

When I get home the recording has captured the life and contrast I'm hoping for. The woodpecker sounds are realistic and have a full tone, even a musical quality. The occasional burst of quacking from some distant mallard ducks adds to the gentle ambience of the river. I'm pleased with it. ◀) 2.7

13 FEBRUARY: When we walk by a river or in the woods, we hear what musician and sound recordist Bernie Krause calls a "soundscape". Although it may be possible to concentrate on the call of one bird at a time, there will always be other sounds in the background. We tend to filter these out of our hearing in real time, but anyone who tries to make a recording of natural sounds will discover how hard it is to avoid capturing extraneous noises. Background sounds can be very distracting when playing back

the recording afterwards, especially if they're made by humans and machinery.

There are three types of sound in a soundscape: 'geophony', caused by natural forces such as wind, water and thunder; 'biophony', created by living things other than humans; and 'anthrophony', specifically the sound of humans and their activities. The first two were around for millions of years before humans came along. The volume and reach of the third increases exponentially with each decade.

I'm lucky that there are quiet and accessible woods in this area. Even so, I can spend hours trying to make recordings of birdsong and still end up with only a minute or two of uninterrupted natural sounds. The majesty of a dawn chorus at 4.30am is regularly marred by the roar of traffic or a passing plane. The stretch of river between Oundle and Cotterstock has a busy road not too far away. Most of the time it's muffled and quiet, but a lot depends on the wind and temperature. It's often more intrusive in the evenings. I can usually filter it out while I'm walking, but at times it's a constant irritant.

Aircraft and traffic sounds affect wildlife too. There's research to show that kingfishers in a noisy roadside environment change the pitch of their calls to make themselves easier to hear. I often detect cries of alarm from birds deep in the forest that have been triggered by the sudden snarl of a distant motorbike. And I was once in a wood when a fast military jet flew over so low that I could see the pilot was wearing shades. In the middle of a quiet afternoon the jet's sudden blast of sound set off a startling rerun of a dawn chorus at full volume.

I find it difficult to cope with the noise when I visit a big city. Among the innate fears we are born with is the fear of loud sounds. Lorries, cars, motorbikes, planes and helicopters all affect our nervous systems, even if we think we're used to them. Natural sounds of that volume would usually signal danger. They'd be the roars of wild animals or the crash of falling trees or boulders. The constant drone of traffic might be a dangerous waterfall. The clang of a metal skip hitting the road could be thunder. In the human world noise is associated with progress, but it's an insidious threat to the whole environment that's not often acknowledged.

14 FEBRUARY: It's Valentine's Day. The wind has veered to the south and the forecast is for much warmer weather. There should much more birdsong and early nesting behaviour in the next few days.

As a child I was told that Valentine's Day happened on 14 February because that's when the birds pair up for the spring. Now I know that some species show signs of pairing as early as January, and many migrant birds won't hook up until they arrive here in April or May. But mid-February isn't a bad time to choose as a turning point for the seasons. Green shoots are beginning to grow up through the forest floor. Birdsong is getting louder and more diverse. Birds are beginning to have mating on their minds.

In parts of medieval Europe mid-February was celebrated as the beginning of spring. In Slovenia it still is today. The ancient Romans had a celebration of human fertility called Lupercalia at the same time of year. It's not obvious that St Valentine himself had any connection to romantic love, but his saint's day coincided with both the folklore and the Roman celebrations. The day itself has been commercialised over the centuries, but doves and flowers are still central to its symbolism.

15 FEBRUARY: A week ago the meadows were still flooded and there looked to be no end to the cold easterly winds. But this morning there's a sepia softness to the meadows and the faintest smell of warm, wet earth. The floods are gone and a south wind is forecast. My shoulders are relaxed as I walk. There's no hurry to get back to shelter. I feel a sense of relief. Winter may not be over quite yet, but it's losing its grip.

I stand opposite the woods by the river and listen as the birds start to sing again after a tough few days. There's a chaffinch, woodpeckers calling and drumming, a single song thrush and an argumentative flock of starlings. It's a pleasure to just stand and drink it all in.

18 FEBRUARY: There is a female stonechat near Cotterstock lock this morning. They're delightful little birds that I associate more with the coast. They seem to turn up every now and then, perching out in the open for minutes at a time on reeds and fence posts. Their feathers are subtle shades of orange and smoky brown, and they make little clacking calls like two pebbles being brushed together.

20 FEBRUARY: I hear a kingfisher calling and see its reflection coming towards me on the surface of the river. As it flies by, I look up to try and see the bird itself, but it becomes invisible among the blur of shapes and shadows on the far bank. It makes me realise I'd have been better off concentrating on the reflection, rather than trying to spot the real thing.

It gets me thinking about reflections and reality, and the other-worldliness of some nature experiences by the river. A tune and some lyrics start to play in my mind as I walk, and by the time I get home a chorus has formed:

Kingfisher blue, I came looking for you
Brilliant blue, lit up by the sun
And you called as you flew, kingfisher blue
And you and the river were one
You and the river were one

I go into my studio and record a quick demo of it with the guitar. I can never tell when an idea for a song or tune will appear. It's always good to note it down as soon as possible.

25 FEBRUARY: I leave home and drive for a few minutes to Glapthorn Cow Pastures. It's a patch of woodland that's managed by the Wildlife Trust for Beds, Cambs and Northants and designated as a Site of Special Scientific Interest. At another time of year I might come here to look for rare black hairstreak butterflies or listen for nightingales. Today I'm searching for peace.

I arrive in late afternoon and stay till dusk. At the far end by the pond there's a special place for listening. Tall, spindly ash trees and broad oaks lift and shape the woodland sounds. It could almost be a church. I sit on a log, stock still, lower my eyes and listen. A robin fetches up with a high, chattering burst of song, hoping to see me off. There are other calls from trees all around: the rattle of a wren, the yaffle of a green woodpecker and the hoots of a tawny owl. A succession of blackbirds flies down to wash at the pond in a quiet flurry of feathers and clucks.

As light fades the wood stills. Then a few distant cries of rooks begin to float across the valley from Southwick, getting steadily louder till a hundred or more circle overhead. One group at a time peels off and perches in trees close by. At first their ratchety calls set off the robins again, but night soon settles and it's quiet once more. A lone frog croaks as the moon rises. A sudden breeze rustles like a round of applause. I walk back through the darkened wood with peace in my heart, a head full of natural sounds, and a deep sense of gratitude.

28 FEBRUARY: I spot a kingfisher from the bridge, perching low on the roots of a willow tree. It sits quietly without trying to catch any fish. It may have already eaten its fill and be taking time to digest its catch. It starts opening and closing its beak, and heaves up a white pellet of undigested fish scales and bones. Every few minutes it ejects a quick spurt of white guano into the water below.

It starts stretching its wings back behind it while fanning the feathers, so from the side it looks like a magnificent brooch crafted in sapphire and jade. Then it holds out one wing at a time, carefully preening and rearranging the feathers with its beak. It starts close to its body then works right out to the end of each wing tip. After that it smooths its head by tucking it under each wing in turn.

Kingfishers need to keep their feathers in good condition for flying and diving into the water. They help insulate against the cold and damp, and display is important now the mating season is starting. The colours need to be bright when competing for a mate, and they make it easier for the pair to spot each other as they work together to raise and feed their chicks.

The kingfisher I'm watching has stayed in the same place for half an hour without showing any sign of wanting to move. It's a privilege to be able to observe it in such a relaxed state. We've been through some fierce weather since the start of the year, but things are looking up. The birds are singing louder with each lengthening day, and the daffodils are out. After straining for so long to catch brief glimpses of those orange and blue feathers, it seems a shame to walk away from this encounter. I'm reluctant to go, but have other things to do. I nod in farewell, and head for home. We'll both be back another day.

MARCH

Fieldfares   Swans   Finding feathers
A pair of kingfishers   Blackbirds
The spirit of the river   Kingfisher nests   Red kite   Chiffchaffs
Mistle thrush   Standing guard   Finding the nest
Dance of the swans   Blackcap   Dawn chorus

1 MARCH: I'm walking through the woods and there's what sounds like a stream tinkling in the distance. It seems odd because there's no stream in that direction. As I get closer, I realise it's the echoing cackle of a big flock of fieldfares perched high in the treetops. They're very loud indeed, and I'm not the only one who's noticed. The resident blue tits hop about from branch to branch, a chaffinch puffs out his pink chest, wrens rattle out expletives and a woodpecker takes out its fury on the nearest tree trunk. Then small groups of fieldfares start to leave the trees and fly out of the woods. The cacophony gradually fades until all I can hear is the scratchy chatter of individual calls as they head out across the fields.

Fieldfares are members of the thrush family, and they migrate here from Scandinavia to take advantage of our milder winters. They arrive in October or November and maraud across the fields and hedgerows like an invading guerrilla army, seeking out red hawthorn berries and worms. Sometimes they gather in trees, and their combined calls can take on a rhythm of their own. I once looked up in wonder towards a flock that sounded like an idling tractor. In the next few weeks they'll start to fly back east as the weather improves on their breeding grounds.

3 MARCH: There's been a family of swans with three cygnets near Snipe Meadow since last year. The young birds are getting more independent, and they look fully grown, but they still haven't developed the pure white plumage of an adult. This morning, the youngsters are standing on their own as I walk right up to them on the path. At first they hiss and stiffen, but soon relax again and go back to preening themselves. One opens out a wing and I realise for the first time how beautifully varied the juvenile feathers are. Each row has a different length, shape and texture. The colours go from browns and greys to subtle tones of violet and peach. The sun picks out rainbows in the tiny pearls of water that nestle in the down on their backs.

I once found a thin scattering of kingfisher feathers by the river, miniature specks of blue and orange against the green of the grass. My excitement soon turned to sadness. It was in July, and they'd probably come from a chick that had been killed by a sparrowhawk. I went home and came back with a small jewellery box, then gently picked up the feathers and put them inside. There were two from the tail, a few from the orange breast, a couple of delicate plumes from the head and the rest were wing feathers with blue just at the tips. Out in the sunlight they were radiant, but when I took them indoors the colours drained away.

If you look at a close-up photo of a kingfisher taken in good light the colouration is wonderfully varied. There's the orange terracotta of its fluffy breast feathers, which carry on into a small patch just behind its eye. Beneath its chin and on the sides of the neck are bright flashes of white. Some of the wing feathers are a dark blue, but others are lighter and even appear green in certain lights. Small circular shapes also adorn the head and wing feathers, so there appears to be a network of tiny turquoise beads.

The orange feathers owe their colour to a pigment, but the blue ones don't. The illusion of colour is created by tiny nanostructures that scatter light like a prism and reinforce the blue portion of the spectrum. This changes with the angle of the light falling on them so they can appear to be different hues. If there's no direct sunlight they can be dark and undistinguished. There may be no colour showing at all.

4 MARCH: It's been cloudy for a few days now, and the low light has made it difficult to take photos. I've seen a kingfisher almost every day but they've been whizzing by at high speed rather than perching.

This afternoon is a lot brighter, so I grab the camera and head for the river. I'm glad I do, because I get a shot of a pair of kingfishers about fifteen feet up in a willow tree by the weir. They perch quietly on neighbouring branches then fly off in close formation along the stream that goes round to the other side of Cotterstock lock.

There is a lot of calling as they disappear into the distance. Often kingfishers give a single call every forty yards or so as they fly, which stops when they land. Counting calls can give you a rough idea of how far they have gone and whether it's worth setting off after them. But in this case the sounds continue till they fade in the distance, so I set off back home.

5 MARCH: I'm standing in the garden, watching a pair of blackbirds build a nest. The actual work is done by the female. She

is very industrious, foraging at the bottom of the garden in old flowerpots for dead stems and grasses, then flying with them into a box hedge. The male keeps a beady eye from a nearby roof and occasionally uses his orange beak to preen his glossy black feathers. Neither bird seems bothered by my presence. Both are focussed in their different ways on the job in hand.

I really love blackbird song. ◀) 3.8 Of all the sounds of spring it's the one I look forward to most, and I can't imagine a dawn or evening chorus at that time of year without it. There's one singing outside the kitchen window on most days now, and it's the perfect accompaniment to making breakfast or washing up. It has a special languid warmth to it, and a tone that's close to some human sounds. One windy day in the depths of winter I was surprised to hear what sounded like a blackbird singing in the distance. It turned out to be a gardener whistling while he worked on his vegetable patch.

Edward Grey, an eminent politician and birdwatcher in the early twentieth century, wrote a lovely book called *The Charm Of Birds*. In it he says: "The songs of other birds please and delight us, but that of the blackbird seems to make a direct appeal to us and stirs some inward emotion." Another great nature writer of the same period, W.H. Hudson, described it as being "nearer to human music than any other bird songs".

Birds with low-pitched songs evolved their tone and timbre so the sound would carry in dense woods and forests. It's only in the last few hundred years that blackbirds have become associated with towns. The number of bird tables in urban gardens means territories can be smaller. At dusk blackbirds may be singing from several roofs in the same street.

Their sound is the essence of spring and early summer, but they only sing at full volume for four months or so. In autumn and winter they can sometimes be heard singing very quietly in evergreen trees and hedges. That's called subsong, and it's a form of practice for the next spring. They hide while they do it, and the sound is so tiny that very few people notice.

6 MARCH: I've been thinking a lot lately about what the river means to me. Walking by it helps me keep fit. Watching and listening to the wildlife has become an essential part of who I am, spiritually and emotionally. At key points in my life I've stood on the riverbank at night and shouted to the stars in sorrow or exultation. I wonder what sort of rituals and beliefs were held by others who lived and walked here in the past? What might the river have meant to them?

I get in the car and drive along the A605 towards Peterborough. Just before it crosses the A1 the road comes to the top of a hill. The broad, flat canvas of the Fens rolls out ahead, and the windscreen fills with sky. I drive round the Peterborough bypass, take the slipway into Fengate industrial estate, then take a right turn by the power station onto a road that passes open fields of grazing horses and pull in at Flag Fen. The journey's taken less than half an hour. I've driven fifteen miles by road, but I've travelled three-and-a-half thousand years back in time.

Flag Fen is named after the yellow flag (or yellow iris) flowers which grow near water. It isn't far from the Nene, and at different times in history parts of the river have run through it. At one time, it will also have been surrounded by saltwater tidal creeks coming inland from the Wash. It's the site of a Bronze Age wooden causeway which was built on the western edge of the Fens and discovered in 1982 by archaeologist Francis Pryor. Most of it is still underground, preserved by the damp peaty soil. It's more than half a mile long, built from over sixty thousand wooden posts and a quarter of a million planks. It was used by herders to drive their animals onto grazing pastures, but objects found during excavations have led experts to believe that it also had a religious and spiritual significance.

Parts of the site are open to the public, and as I walk across the car park into the teeth of a bitter, rain-flecked wind a kestrel flies by with a whinnying call and lands on the roof of a reconstructed round house. Its mauve and chestnut feathers stand out against the weathered green of the turf. A section of the excavated causeway is under the cover of a specially designed floating building, and inside it the tops of ancient wooden posts stick out of deep water that is replenished by taps dripping to retain humidity and stop them drying out. The sounds of the water drops echo and merge like a drone of ancestral voices. Looking down onto a surface broken by moving concentric ripples, I'm reminded that before the advent of shiny metal surfaces in around 100BC the only way a person could see their own reflection was to look into still water.

Water and wetlands seem to have become important spiritual and religious places after about 1500BC. They represented boundaries, liminal spaces on the edge of the land that were portals to the worlds inhabited by gods or ancestors. People threw or placed votive offerings into rivers and wet places. The superstition lives on in the custom of throwing coins into a fountain.

Many objects have been found in the sediments at Flag Fen. There are weapons, tools and jewellery. Bronze swords had been deliberately broken and the parts placed together in the water. They were too valuable for it to have been accidental. There have been other finds that shed light on different aspects of daily life at Flag Fen. There's the oldest complete wooden wheel in England, and boats carved out of single logs were discovered at nearby Must Farm. People travelled about, and this culture was likely to be very similar to that further upriver in places like Oundle.

As I drive back home, I think about the people who lived in the Roman town close to the meadows where I walk every day. Their culture revered water, and they shared with the Ancient Greeks the belief that you had to cross the River Styx to get to the afterlife. To prepare for that they were buried with a coin to pay the ferryman. It's striking that many local village churches were built close to the river, including Wadenhoe, Cotterstock, Tansor and Fotheringhay. Could they have been sited in places that already had a spiritual use before the arrival of Christianity?

There was plenty of scope for legends and stories in the way the river affected the people who lived along it. Sources bubbled up from the ground as springs and journeyed to the sea. A river could be difficult or dangerous to cross. Water brought life, but it also brought floods and drowning. People who travelled on the river in boats could be traders or invaders.

On a practical level the river provided fish and wildfowl to eat. It brought drinking water for people and their livestock, and was used for cooking and washing. Receding floods would leave a layer of silt on fields and meadows, making them more fertile. Watermills could provide power for grinding corn. The river was important for transport before there were good roads. At first rafts or boats could simply drift downstream. Later there were rudimentary sails, punting poles and paddles, and boats towed by men or horses. There's a record from 1648 of a boat taking a cargo of cheese along the river from Peterborough to Higham Ferrers. It was the cheapest from of transport even though they had to unload and manhandle the boat around sixteen obstacles along the way.

As boats developed, the need to transport goods like coal spurred the river authorities to improve and slow the river with locks and weirs. It became fully navigable from Northampton to the sea in 1761. Unfortunately the growth of industry and population also meant that it became a main drain for human and manufacturing waste. The tanneries serving the traditional shoe towns of Northamptonshire upstream severely damaged the ecology of the river, and the chemical run-off from treated fields made things even worse.

Today the river has been tamed and most people use it for well-being and leisure. But it's still part of our spiritual landscape. Modern life threatens its fragile ecosystem, and now more than ever it's important to respect and look after it.

11 MARCH: This morning, I walk the first part of the riverbank with a strong westerly roaring in my ears, wondering where kingfishers might go to fish out of the wind. It seems likely they'll be on the stretch that's sheltered by the wood.

I hear some calling the moment I get there, and it soon becomes a stream of urgent syncopated notes. ◀ 3.9 It takes a while to pick out a bird on the far bank, but suddenly there it is, a familiar blue shape half-hidden among the willow twigs. Then another flies by and they both disappear into some ivy. They are fishing alright, but for each other, giddy as teenagers at a school disco, flitting high into the trees, waiting, then chasing, then hiding again.

It must be a pair. Both sexes guard their territory, so if they were two unrelated males or females they would have chased each other faster and further to try and drive away an intruder. This is coy stuff, delightful to watch. I stay for several minutes then walk on and leave them to it.

12 MARCH: Common kingfishers are unusual birds in that they create their nests by tunnelling into the vertical earth banks of a river or stream. They start to make a hole by flying at the bank with their beaks, then make it deeper by pecking at the earth and scrabbling it out behind them with their short tails and feet. When the tunnel is two or three feet long, they open out the far end into a wider nest chamber where the eggs will be laid. It's a long, exhausting job, and they may have to restart further along the bank if they encounter stones or tree roots as they dig. The opening is usually about eighteen inches below the top of the bank, but at the same time it needs to be far enough above the water to avoid being flooded. It keeps the chicks safe from most predators, though they're not protected from rats and snakes, and mink are known to dig down from above.

Today I see a kingfisher perched in a sheltered spot just upstream of the weir. It's in a dense mass of ivy which covers a small tree right at the edge of the river. I watch for several minutes before it makes a short dive into the water then flies back into the ivy and stays hidden. On my way back, I pass the same spot and hear two kingfishers calling before they suddenly fly out and vanish upriver.

It's possible they will choose to nest here as there's plenty of cover for them, but the bank isn't high enough to dig a nest hole without the risk of flooding. The path is close by too, but kingfishers aren't always shy. I once noticed a nest hole in a riverbank right next to a busy car park by the River Thames near Oxford. People were putting canoes in the water just beneath it while children and dogs splashed about in the shallows. Every now and then a blue-feathered blur darted into the nest with a fish. No one else appeared to notice.

13 MARCH: There's a small dead tree by the river which I always glance at as I pass. Today I spot a bright patch of red on it that shapeshifts into a great spotted woodpecker. It's unaware of me as it spirals endlessly up and down and around the branches, and I can just about hear its beak quietly tapping for grubs and insects. Usually I see woodpeckers much higher in the treetops, and have to crane my neck to see them. But this is at eye level and much easier to watch.

In the woods on the way back I notice the large, angular shape of a red kite flying low towards the river. There's a loud splash as it plunges into the water and flies off holding a silver fish in its talons. It all happens so fast that my first impulse is to doubt what I'd seen. Surely red kites are carrion eaters, feeding on roadkill and the corpses of small animals? Could it have been an osprey? But there is no mistaking the shape, size and colour of the bird. It has to be a red kite.

When I get home I look it up, and find that kites are known to prey on dead or dying fish floating close to the surface. The following day I bump into a dog walker who's a member of the local golf club. He says that it is common to see kites circling the lake on the golf course and swooping down to strike at the water. Half-eaten scraps of fish and bones are often left around the shore.

18 MARCH: Chiffchaffs have been flitting about in the woods for a few days now, and this morning there are brief bursts of song. Though some spend the winter here it seems likely that migrants are arriving from Africa. That's a proper sign of spring. There are others too. I see my first yellow brimstone butterfly of the year in the woods, and there are wild violets opening up by the path. Some clumps have white flowers.

To me the chiffchaff's call is special. Most bird sounds are urgent and declamatory, and the volume comes and goes. Chiffchaffs set up a steady rhythm as if they are calling their own name over and over. The sound seems to come from high in the treetops, like an urgent and ever-present Greek chorus commenting on the forest below. Gilbert White noted that: "it utters two sharp, piercing notes, so loud in hollow woods as to occasion an echo..." For a small bird it makes a big sound that carries a surprisingly long way. 🔊 3.10

19 MARCH: Today the river tells a tale of two seasons. On the meadow bank the wind is cold as flint. I see just one bird, a chiffchaff hiding in the reeds. The only sounds are high winds and fast-flowing water. On the way back a small patch of grass is sheltered by a belt of trees and slopes towards the sun. It is warm and calm, full of the songs of spring: wrens, robins, goldfinches and the cheery shouts of a green woodpecker.

20 MARCH: Yesterday's nagging northeasterly has gone. There's just the occasional gentle breeze ruffling through the reeds by the

river. I stop to listen as a mistle thrush starts to sing from high in the trees. My heart soars.

There's no point in looking for him with the naked eye, and anyway that would be a waste of good listening time. The mistle thrush is a sonic mystery I hope never to solve. There's something about the sound of those few repeated notes, the call and response, that stops me in my tracks. I just have to listen.

When I do a recording of music or birdsong I spend a lot of time trying to make it appear natural. Microphones never capture the sound as it really is, and the trick is to reproduce what your ears actually heard at the time, rather than what the technology has captured in the first instance.

This may involve changing the balance of frequencies by taking away high or low sounds to get a better balance and tone. It may also mean adding small amounts of reverberation or echo to give a sense of the space the sound was made in. The point in saying all this is that the mistle thrush's song appears to have come through the mixing desk of a celestial sound engineer. Subtle work has been done which I can't quite fathom. The result is magical. 🔊 3.11

With other birds a large part of the beauty comes from the echoing sounds of the woods and spaces around them. Owls and cuckoos appear flat and scratchy when you hear them up close, but wonderfully rich from a distance when the vibrations are bouncing around among the trees. It's the same with woodpeckers. But to me mistle thrushes still have that strange, haunting, skirling quality whether they are calling from high up in a wood, a single tree at the roadside or perched on the aerial of a city office block. Like other birds they exploit the acoustics to get their point across, but there's something else going on that's wonderful and inexplicable.

The country name for the bird is the 'stormcock', because it sometimes sings early in the year in wild and stormy weather. There's an emotion there, a yearning, more of a cry than a call. Someone once described it as sounding like it had forgotten the words and was trying to remember them.

The thrush stops singing, and I linger for a while before carrying on with my walk. I can't get that sound out of my head. I wouldn't want to. But as I near home I can hear young children playing in the pocket park. That begins to take over my listening ear and makes me smile with pleasure.

22 MARCH: I'm walking downstream from the bridge and a kingfisher passes by going the other way. It looks to have landed near the school boathouses. I turn round to go back, expecting it to have gone by the time I get near. But it stays put for quite a while, perched on the top rail of a weathered wooden fence that juts out over the water. The bridge is just beyond it, and the bird is beautifully framed by the curved brick and stone background of one of the arches.

It's a male, and he appears to be guarding his territory. He flies off under the bridge and then comes back through and hovers for a few seconds above the water. Then he whizzes off downstream. A passing walker tells me he saw two kingfishers fighting here yesterday. They'd flown directly at each other with a huge amount of noisy calling, and even collided at one point. Rosemary Eastman describes something similar in her book. She watched two males flying at each other. Each was trying to knock the other into the water. In a fight to the death one would hold the other's beak under the water till it drowned.

I'd suspected that the bridge might mark the border between two territories, and the fighting might confirm that. I turn to go back through the meadows, and just as I reach the wood a kingfisher zooms by from behind me. It's carrying a fish in its beak. Normally when they catch their prey they grasp it by its middle or tail and quickly make for a nearby perch. Then they beat the fish against a branch to break the bones and spines before swallowing it head first. But when they're feeding young, they fly back to the nest holding the fish with the tail right back within their mouths and the head protruding from the tip. That way they can present them straight into the beaks of the chicks.

But it's far too early for chicks. I haven't even seen signs of nesting yet. Male kingfishers feed their partners as part of courtship, which may be immediately followed by mating. It's a way for the female to judge the male's suitability as a partner, and it strengthens the bond between them. It also helps her put on weight before laying eggs. The bird carrying the fish flies towards the trees downstream and there are excitable calls from further in. I don't actually see courtship feeding happening, but everything seems to point towards it.

When I get home, I go straight to Rosemary Eastman's book. The kingfishers she was watching in 1963 had already been digging their nest since the last week in February. It's possible that's happening locally and I've missed it. But what really chimes with what I've just seen is that she witnessed courtship feeding on 22 March, the same day as today.

24 MARCH: I've found a kingfisher's nest! After hearing a lot of kingfisher calls coming from a bend in the stream that runs from

the weir to below the lock, I quietly enter a copse and peer through a gap in the reeds. I am just in time to see a bird fly at the bank and disappear into a hole. The other half of the pair carries on calling from somewhere nearby. After a minute or two the first bird tumbles out of the hole backwards. It quickly recovers itself in mid-air and flies off.

Coming out backwards indicates that the tunnel is only just wide enough to let the birds in to dig. They haven't yet made the wider nesting chamber that would enable them to turn around inside. Later, when there are chicks, there will be droppings coming from the hole itself. For now there are some by a perch just to the right where the adults have been resting between bouts of digging.

I don't stay long so as not to alarm them. Researchers and photographers sometimes set up hides near nests, but I wouldn't consider doing that. The nest is close to a public footpath and there would be a danger of attracting attention to the birds. It's also illegal to closely watch or disturb a kingfisher's nest without a special licence. Instead, I find a spot behind some tall reeds about fifty yards upstream where I'll be able to check on its progress every few days.

I walk further downriver, and when I return things have quietened down. Later I see a bird carrying a fish into the woods nearby, and there are a lot of calls as it arrives. Courtship and mating seem to be carrying on at the same time as the nest building.

27 MARCH: I'm watching a pair of swans on the stream near the weir. They start off by swimming side by side, stationary in the current, not far away from me but completely oblivious to my presence. Then they begin to arch their necks and dip their heads into the water in unison. Occasionally they face each other and

touch beaks so the curve of their necks resembles a heart shape. Then they repeatedly brush water back along their bodies. The movements are wonderfully slow and gentle, like a beautiful balletic courtship dance. It's almost as if they are performing to music.

28 MARCH: Overnight, the clock moved forwards to British Summer Time. Every year at this time I go to the woods at Glapthorn Cow Pastures to record the dawn chorus. This morning I set out early and put on BBC Radio 3 in the car. There's a sitar playing a morning raga, an improvisation based on a special scale to reflect and honour the mood of daybreak.

The birds have just started singing when I get to the wood. It's misty, and there are dewdrops hanging from the twigs amid the pearl-coloured blossom on the blackthorn. A blackbird is calling by the entrance. There are song thrushes and wrens on both sides as I walk along the rides. In the past I've spent so many hours listening and recording in this sound world, with its open scrubby spaces at the bottom and the tall thin ash trees higher up the slope. Hearing these sounds bouncing around the woods is like listening to an old friend speak, a whole gathering of friends talking together. I'm starting to get my ears back in tune, listening to what they're saying.

I set up my recording gear, this time with the microphones clipped inside a parabolic dish that focusses and lifts the sound. As I listen through the headphones there are blackbirds and song thrushes at the centre, and wrens, robins, chiffchaffs and a chaffinch off to the sides. In the distance there are a few hoots from tawny owls, a green woodpecker's call and some drumming from its great spotted cousin. There's the tiny thistly sound of a treecreeper too, and the '*dit dit dit*' of a nuthatch as rooks caw overhead. ◀ 3.12

It sounds like a good healthy dawn chorus, with all the songs I'd expect before the next group of spring migrants arrive. Sheep and cattle noises from the neighbouring farm start to filter through, and there are a few whinnies from a horse and cackles of farmyard geese. As I leave the wood and cross the road to my car there's the familiar sound of a Land Rover towing a clackety trailer along a distant gravel track. The day's woken up, and all sounds right with the world.

29 MARCH: This morning at Cotterstock millpond I hear my first blackcap of the year. It's a glorious fanfare for spring that lifts my spirits every time I hear it. It starts with a sound like water spitting on a hotplate, then morphs into beautiful bright strings of melody that always end in an uplift. 🔊 3.13

As I walk past a barn that's being renovated, someone calls out my name. He explains that he is related by marriage to Phil Rudkin, who has asked to be remembered to me. Phil is a skilled and knowledgeable birdsong recordist. I remember going to a talk he gave in the village hall about twenty years ago when I was first starting to record nightingales. He was an inspiration at the time, and afterwards I walked back along the starlit track to Oundle buzzing with excitement. On the few occasions when our paths have crossed since, Phil would generously share his knowledge and encouragement.

It seems fitting to be reminded of Phil just after hearing the first blackcap of the year, so when I get home I contact him. He says the blackcap is his favourite singer: "Its song is pure music... it starts simply and builds into a melody that rises and falls, and has what I would call a coda ending, just like in music." As a young man, Phil was very interested in wildlife and did some bird surveys for the British Trust for Ornithology. Then in 1966 he went to a meeting of the newly formed Rutland Natural History Society. During the evening they watched *The Woodpeckers of the Black Forest*, and Phil described its effect as "mind boggling". The atmosphere in the hall was "ecstatic", and he felt that "my new journey had begun!"

After a period leading annual dawn-chorus surveys, Phil bought his first tape recorder in 1973. He used his own recordings to teach bird-recognition evening classes and eventually went on to win national and international awards for recordings of seals and woodpeckers. And through all that time he worked tirelessly to document local birds and insects. For me Phil epitomises the sort of person who takes such a delight in nature that it can't fail to be passed on to others. His proudest moment was being elected chairman of the Natural History Society he'd joined two decades previously.

31 MARCH: The temperature's been rising for a few days now, and this afternoon it's going to reach twenty degrees Celsius. The air smells of cut grass and warm earth. The first bluebells are out in the woods and buttercups are dotted about in the meadows. Marsh marigolds light the way along the muddy path through the trees by the river, and two butterflies have settled in the sun on a rough wooden fence by Cotterstock Mill. One, a comma, is holding its quivering orange tiger-print wings outstretched. The other butterfly, a peacock, has its wings folded above its body like a dark leaf. Then it suddenly opens them, and displays warm reds and yellows dusted with the icy blue of its eye spots.

In the reeds upstream of the kingfishers' nest I find a spot to sit and listen out for their calls. At first there's just the gentle sound of water lapping, but then I hear the kingfishers coming with a high repeated two-note "*tzee-tzoo... tzee-tzoo*". It starts off quiet and thin, then gets louder as they fly along the stream from the right.

One flashes past and settles in the distance near the hole. I can hear the other calling from further up the bank. A stuttering blizzard of piccolo-like pips passes between them that sounds like an almighty argument. Then they take off and fly away downstream, calling as they go.

The sheer speed of their sound and movements is disorientating, but the fact that I heard them both together suggests that they're not sitting on the eggs yet. I'd expect things to be quieter when that happens, with one member of the pair staying in the nest at any one time.

It's thrilling to watch and listen while their story unfolds. As I walk home along the river there's a wonderful range of birdsong from the trees on the far bank. Butterflies are flitting in the sun by the path. The dun, camouflaged tones of the winter landscape are beginning to change to different shades of green, and there's more light and colour every day. There's every chance that adult kingfishers will be out on a branch with their chicks here before too long, a rare and beautiful sight with its own special name: 'a crown of kingfishers'.

APRIL

Home thoughts   Barnwell kingfishers   The fox and the owl
The repair workshop   The Rothschilds   Willow warblers
Swallows and snipe   Cuckoo and nightingale
Reed warbler   St George's Day   Meeting a bird ringer   Bluebells

1 APRIL: I first heard Robert Browning's poem *Home Thoughts from Abroad* when I was ten. A very enthusiastic young student teacher read it to our class, and I remember being puzzled by the first line: "Oh, to be in England now that April's there…" He'd probably chosen the poem because our school was on a military airbase and most pupils had lived overseas, but I was too young to really understand it. At the time, I didn't have much grasp of what the seasons meant. There was either good weather when you played outside, or bad when you played indoors. And I'd just got back from living in Norway for two-and-a-half years. If you'd asked me what I'd missed about England when I was there, I'd have been hard put to say. But now I was back in England, playing in the school football team and watching *Top of the Pops* every week. I'd have certainly missed that if I'd had to live abroad again.

But I remember him reading the poem and trying to explain it to us, and liking the bit about the "wise thrush; he sings each song twice over". Now I can appreciate the whole poem much more. Browning was living in Italy at the time and missing the unfolding subtleties of an English spring that can take weeks and months to arrive: the tiny unfurling leaves, the "blossoms and dewdrops" and the morning fields "rough with hoary dew" that will be transformed "when noontide wakes anew". I've come to relish the slowness of that process, and if there's a sudden warm spell and all the leaves come out at once I can even feel a twinge of sadness. I've waited so long through the winter that I want to savour the gradual transition to spring. It needs to happen at walking speed, not in haste.

I feel the same about the arrival of the migrant birds from Africa. I'm happy to hear the chiffchaffs and blackcaps in late March, but then prefer to wait a while for the first willow warbler, followed by the swallows, cuckoos, nightingales, reed warblers, swifts and spotted flycatchers. Sometimes during a late spring many can arrive in the same week, and for me that causes a sensory overload. If that's a problem for me, imagine the problems native birds have in dealing with a sudden influx of unfamiliar visitors noisily competing for food and territory.

Bird migration is a fascinating thing. Migrations of people are now generally in one direction, but for birds there's a seasonal movement from one part of the world to another and then back again. Species will only migrate if it's in their interest to do so. They usually fly to where there's enough food in spring to breed and raise their young. Good timing is important. Migrant birds need to wait until the weather is good enough to provide enough food, but make sure there's still time to breed and moult before they have to leave again. There's a great deal of energy and risk involved. Most species travel by night when the air is cooler and more humid. It's thought that they may navigate by the moon and stars. Males usually travel ahead so they can stake out their territories, then sing to attract the females when they arrive later.

Every year I'm nervous that some species of bird won't make it here from Africa. They're such delicate creatures, and they have to fly thousands of miles through droughts and storms, not to mention the dangers from human hunting and pollution. There may also be overdevelopment in the areas where they traditionally rest to build up body fat for their journeys, meaning less food to fuel travel. If they don't arrive locally, I can usually drive somewhere else in the area to hear a cuckoo or a nightingale. But I really want to experience them on my own patch, as part of the warp and weft of the landscape I know so well.

2 APRIL: I decide to walk to Barnwell Park to see what's going on with the wildlife there. It's no accident that the coffee shop is called The Kingfisher Café. Customers on the decking are sometimes treated to the sight of the birds flashing across the water in front of them.

It's a bright, sunny day but there are black clouds blowing in from the north, and there's a sudden wintry flurry of snow as I arrive. Although I don't usually enjoy waiting about in bird hides, I duck into one for shelter. It's very calming inside, sitting on my own out of the wind in a wooden hut filled with the scent of fresh pine timber. I watch the snowflakes slanting across a small patch of water edged with reeds and trees. There are no birds to be seen, though I can hear nuthatches calling. The sight of the falling snow starts to make me feel a bit sleepy.

I suddenly sit upright. A kingfisher has landed on a perch just in front of me, no more than twenty feet away, so close that the colours are radiant even in the low light. It peers down into the water, then makes an unsuccessful dive for a fish and flies up again to another branch. The snow's starting to fade now. There's a quiet call from another kingfisher hidden further away in the reed beds. As I move across the hide to try and get a better look, the nearest bird lets out an answering call and flies off towards it.

I leave the hide and go round to the other side of the water, walking to where the kingfisher was headed. There's a play park close by. I can hear children's voices, and a squeaky swing that sounds like a goose honking. The sun comes out again. I soon pick out the glow of a tiny blue shape on a branch facing away from me. It flies to a stump in the water then angles upwards into a tall willow tree. There's another call as its mate arrives on a branch close by. I can see through my camera that one has the black beak of a male while the other has the orange markings of a female. They stretch up their necks to elongate their bodies, then both fly towards the stream that flows round the edge of the park, twittering all the while.

I walk home thinking about the different sounds they were making. They were quieter, more conversational, designed to be heard from close to. The calls were two-toned and clipped, almost '*sszipp! szoo!*' It looks like I've discovered another courting couple.

3 APRIL: The evenings are lighter now, and I walk out along the Oundle side of the river just before dusk. It feels very different from the morning. The sun hovers above the ridge to the west, and it feels like both the countryside and I are relaxing now the day's nearly done. I'm walking at the edge of a field just outside the wood. A local man once told me he used to find shards of Roman pottery when he played here as a child. A pair of mandarin ducks takes off

from the path and flies into the trees. A curlew makes its swooping melancholic calls as it follows the river downstream.

Near the end of the wood I step in among the trees. During the day it's filled with birdsong, but it's gloomier now. There are calls from a song thrush and robin. I can just make out a tiny goldcrest hopping from twig to twig in a blur of motion and faint thistly sounds. A tawny owl hoots. There's a '*kewick!*' in response from a female owl further away. I've found their beautiful feathers and dry crumbly pellets here in the past. It'll be worth looking again during the day.

The sun's disappeared, though the sky's still bright in the west. The fields and hedgerows are beginning to blur into each other, and sounds become clearer as the sights fade. I make my way carefully back along the path, feeling with my feet as I go, listening to my footsteps on the bare earth. A bat flutters overhead as the owls become more distant. There's the ribald hoot of a moorhen and the rushing sound of the weir. Low in the undergrowth there are furtive rustlings. The day may be ending but the night's only getting started. A new cast of characters is taking over with a soundtrack all of its own.

4 APRIL: I wake at dawn and go up to the woods at Glapthorn. Rays of sunlight pour through the branches and hang on the mist as I walk among the trees. There's still a hint of frost, and steam rises from the green mossy trunk of a fallen oak. The sun throws barred shadows across the grassy ride ahead.

I stand for a while looking at water drops suspended from a blackthorn. I'm fascinated by their glassy brightness, and the tiny upside-down image of the woods that appears within them like in a crystal ball. A woodpecker drums me back to the present. A mistle thrush calls from a tall ash tree by the farm. I have to go home for now but decide to come back later.

As I enter the woods later in the evening the outline of a fox trots across the path ahead and disappears into the trees. Further into the wood, I look along a ride at right angles to the path and he's there again. I sit on a favourite stump for a long time with my eyes closed, listening to the song thrushes and circling rooks and an early tawny owl. Then I open my eyes. The fox is standing stock still on the other side of a clearing, looking straight at me. We hold each other's stares for a few moments. Then he decides I'm neither dangerous nor particularly interesting, shrugs his haunches and takes off with a swish of his gorgeous red brush. I'd been watching him on my way through the woods, but he'd been watching me too.

A few years ago on a dark evening I was sitting with my eyes closed on this very same stump. It's next to an oak tree that's snapped off about fifteen feet above the ground. I heard the scratch and scrape of talons landing on the broken tree directly over my head. Then there was the loud, hoarse cry of a tawny owl. I cringed, feeling the hairs rise on the back of my neck. My heart started to beat loud and fast. This was a little too close for comfort, and I was acutely aware of the soft scalp of my unprotected head. Then I heard the clatter of talons again as it took off and saw a shape flying up through the trees. It was a long time before I stood up. As I walked silently back down the path, I was pleased to hear more hoots, but also glad that they were at a safe distance.

7 APRIL: It's been quieter along the river towards Cotterstock during the last few days, but this morning I spot a lone male

kingfisher perching at the water's edge. I've been used to seeing two together, so the fact that he is on his own could mean that his partner has started to lay eggs in the nest.

Ronald and Rosemary Eastman worked out a way of carefully opening a nest so they could film it from above. That gave them a unique insight into the laying process. After mating with the male, who perches on her back while grasping feathers at the back of her neck, the female might lay an egg each day for six days. She starts to incubate them all at the same time so that they hatch together after about twenty-one days. Both sexes sit on the eggs but the female tends to stay with them at night. The chicks are ready to leave the nest around twenty-five days later.

Whatever stage the local kingfishers have got to, they've been through several heady weeks of defending their territory, seeing off rivals, courting, mating and creating a nest. The nest building itself is exhausting. Both birds peck away at the earth bank like woodpeckers, shovelling the loose soil away behind them with their tail and feet. There may have been false starts. The tunnel might have hit a stone and forced them to abandon it and resume elsewhere. Progress can be as little as a couple of inches a day, and their beaks may be abraded by the work. But they eventually create a tunnel where the eggs can be laid.

Compared to that the next period of sitting on the nest should be relatively quiet and subdued. As the kingfisher flies away I wish him and his partner luck. They've done a lot of work, but there's still plenty more to do.

8 APRIL: I spend today in my workshop repairing and adjusting some instruments. My harp, which I made over thirty years ago, has

developed a crack in the soundbox a couple of inches long, caused by the wood drying out over time. There are little struts glued to the inside that will stop it from getting any worse, but it needs gluing to stabilise it and prevent it affecting the sound. Traditional glues are best for this type of job. They're made from animal hide and need to be warmed up before they can be used. I get out my glue boiler and put some water in along with a handful of glue granules from a big glass jar on the shelf. Then I light a small spirit burner and put it underneath.

Hide glue has a yeasty, soupy smell. I occasionally dip my fingers into the mixture and rub them together to feel the consistency. Too thick, and it won't penetrate the crack in the harp. Too thin, and the joint won't be strong enough. When it feels right I rub glue into the crack with my finger. I squint through a soundhole in the bottom of the instrument to check that the glue has reached through to the other side. Then I wipe away the surplus, and the job is done.

The next task needs a lot more time and thought. I have an acoustic bass guitar which I made at around the same time as the harp. I'd been using it on some recordings but found I couldn't get the tone I was looking for. The problem isn't with the instrument as such, but the technique of playing it. The strings are thick and need to be plucked strongly by the first two fingers on the right hand. But there is no easy way of anchoring my thumb to give a strong and stable hand position. I decide to make a small carved plate and attach it to the instrument where my thumb can rest and have a purchase.

I spend a while drawing a design on paper. It's important that all the parts of an instrument look good and appear to belong together. Then I find a piece of walnut wood about a quarter of an inch thick cut from a local tree that was blown down in a storm. I cut it to a teardrop shape and start to carve away some of the thickness towards the edges. I spend some time getting the edge on the chisel just right, and check it by seeing if it will shave the hair on the back of my wrist. A sharp tool is a joy to use, as it cuts through the wood easily and sticks to the wood. Otherwise there's the danger of it suddenly slipping. That's bad for the woodwork and might cause an injury.

Next I create an indentation where my thumb will rest, shaping the wood so it fits comfortably and sanding away the sharp edges. The dust of each timber has its own distinctive smell, and walnut has a spicy, fruity scent. When the wood is smooth, I take it outside to check under natural light that all the scratches have been taken out, then rub some Danish oil into the surface.

That's when the real beauty of the grain comes out, and it stops becoming a piece of wood and becomes part of an instrument. I attach the thumb plate to the bass and start to play it. The sound is much better: stronger and more musical. It's always good to make something that looks right, but whether it works properly and sounds right is the real test.

It is very satisfying to take an idea from concept to working reality in the space of a couple of hours. Making an instrument from scratch takes weeks and months. There's a lot of waiting for glue to dry, and there are many stages to go through before you can hear what it sounds like. But that's when all that work becomes worthwhile. The inanimate bits of wood come alive, and you can feel the vibrations. You've created something a player can use to express their musical and emotional feelings. It's when the instrument leaves the workshop that its life really starts.

9 APRIL: As far as nature goes, I always work on the assumption that there's a lifetime's worth of experiences still waiting for me within walking distance of my own front door. But today I decide to extend my range and drive to Woodwalton Fen, which is across the county border in Cambridgeshire. On the way I stop off at Ashton, only a mile down the road from Oundle. The village has thatched stone cottages set around a green. Unusually, the pub is named after a butterfly: The Chequered Skipper.

Ashton was built in 1900 by Charles Rothschild, a member of the famous banking family who owned and lived on the estate. He was an amateur entomologist who managed his land to conserve nature and passed on his love of insects and conservation to his daughter Miriam. She lived there until her death in 2005, aged 96. I never met her, but she was a well-known and forceful character, both locally and across the world. She became a leading authority on fleas and published over three hundred scientific papers. But she also had broad interests in wildlife and conservation which she pursued with extraordinary energy and focus. She propagated her own seed mix, which she dubbed "Farmer's Nightmare", to encourage wildflower meadows amongst the "billiard-table" fields of conventional agriculture. I wasn't surprised to find that one of her record choices on *Desert Island Discs* was a recording of a nightingale. She talked on the programme about hearing one sing by her window at Wold House, which was almost hidden behind a mass of ivy, honeysuckle and wisteria.

Charles Rothschild was one of the first people in the UK to realise that conserving habitat was vital to rescue rare and endangered species. He found suitable patches of undeveloped land and started to buy them. When he purchased Wicken Fen in

1899 it became the UK's first nature reserve. He created a list of 284 potential reserves, and the body he set up to achieve this was the forerunner of today's Wildlife Trusts.

The second piece of land he bought was Woodwalton Fen, my intended destination. But first I go for a walk in the beautiful woods at Ashton Wold. The horse chestnut trees have fresh new leaves hanging down from the buds. They have the damp, fragile look of an emerging butterfly's wings. There are primroses by the path and chiffchaffs ringing out overhead. Nuthatches call from lower down. The sounds are echoing through the trees. As the other leaves come out they'll subtly change the echoes, just as they alter the quality of light shining through to the forest floor.

I get back in the car and drive through small stone villages until I reach the flat fields, dykes and skies of Cambridgeshire's Fens. The roads are raised up above the farmland and become straighter but more bumpy. I always get the feeling I'm at sea when driving across the Fens. There's no clear horizon, and the isolated farmhouses could be other boats bobbing about on the surface.

I arrive at Woodwalton Fen. It's a National Nature Reserve, an island of wetland habitat in an ocean of commercial farmland. As I cross a bridge at the entrance, there's the welcoming sound of a kingfisher darting along the banks of the dyke beneath.

During Rothschild's time the reserve would have been much wetter than it is now. He had to use a punt to get around much of it. Drainage of the surrounding fens has dried out the peat. He built a wooden thatched bungalow raised on concrete stilts that's still there today. I sit on the steps to have a drink and a sandwich. There are flood markings painted on the stilts. At different times in the past the water would have come up to my chest.

I set off to explore the reserve. The turf is springy underfoot and releases a spicy camomile scent as I walk. There are ditches full of treacle-coloured peat water fringed with tall reed stalks glowing in the sun. Areas of boggy birch woods with alder catkins and flowering blackthorn have a timeless feel. At the northern edge of the reserve marsh harriers are flying in pairs and nesting in the reed beds. A little grebe and a coot paddle in a small area of open water. A Chinese water deer emerges and stands at the edge of the reeds.

From somewhere close by a bittern booms its remarkable low frequency call. It's not particularly loud, but it can travel for great distances across water. I can hear it all the way back to the car. The pioneering birdsong recordist Ludwig Koch called it a "foghorn-like note, softly struck, but of astonishing carrying power".

On the way home I think about Charles Rothschild travelling back with his young family from Woodwalton to Ashton in the early twentieth century, the boot of their splendid vintage car packed with mahogany boxes containing specimens of rare fenland fleas.

10 APRIL: It's early morning at Glapthorn, and there's the very welcome sound of a newly arrived willow warbler. It has a freewheeling spiral of song which makes me think of a spinning sycamore wing falling to the floor. To me it's a sound that says spring has really arrived. ◀ 4.14 There's also a song thrush in full flow, a lovely strong singer who's found the ideal spot among the thin ash trees to enhance his voice. ◀ 4.15

There's no indication of a nightingale yet, though one could arrive any day now. Nightingales are a favourite subject of composers, writers and poets. The song thrush has elements of the same song, but there's something very special about the nightingale's version.

After an initial period when they first arrive, the birds rarely show themselves. It's magical to hear their loud and virtuosic sound coming from deep in a thicket, especially at night when the rest of the world is silent. I've recorded their songs and listened to them over and over, and it's clear that they never repeat the exact same calls. There's always an embellishment aimed at impressing a female or outperforming a rival male. Often they will sing against each other, trading phrases and trying to better each other through direct imitation.

Part of the nightingale's attraction is that it sings a short burst of song and then leaves a gap before starting up again. The writer H.E. Bates was born and brought up in Rushden, upstream on the River Nene. He wrote of the nightingale's "electric, suspended quality", and how the silences give a sense of "restraint about to be magically broken".

The nightingale isn't a colourful bird, though the feathers have a lovely tinge of auburn in the right light. But its song is full of life, and that more than makes up for it. I once heard a storyteller describing how the birds got their colours. The Creator loaded a palette with the best and brightest colours of the rainbow, then started painting parakeets and parrots in reds and greens and yellows. Then they brushed blue onto the peacocks and kingfishers. Eventually there was only one dowdy little bird left. There was hardly any paint on the palette by now, but all the remaining scraps of rainbow colour were gathered on the tip of a very small brush and used to paint the back of its throat. That bird was the nightingale. 🔊 4.16

12 APRIL: There are two swallows wheeling above Cotterstock millpond this morning. Since last autumn the view across to

St Andrew's church has felt like a still life. Now it's become a movie again as the swallows wheel and dive around its square stone tower.

On the way back to Oundle there's a snipe drumming over Snipe Meadow. It makes a fast circular flight that dips now and then so that its feathers vibrate, or drum, with a thin braying sound. Spinning round to watch it leaves me giddy and excited. It's the first time I've heard one here in about twenty years. I'm itching to tell someone. Luckily a regular walker comes along with his grandson, and I share the experience with them. The boy is about eleven, bright and full of curiosity about why and how the bird is making the sound. It's easy to explain how, but not so easy to explain why. We talk about territory, and about the need to provide food and safety for chicks. It's a useful conversation for me and helps get my thoughts in order too.

I walk on into town to buy an Easter card for my mum. A song thrush is calling loudly from the churchyard. It sounds at first like another is answering it, but then I realise they're echoes bouncing back off the stone wall of the Talbot Hotel. When I get home, I check the bird reports from the south of England. There's an exciting new entry from Sussex: 'Nightingale singing in Abbots Wood at 1 pm today'. They've crossed the Channel. It shouldn't be long before they're here.

14 APRIL: There is a cuckoo singing on the far side of the river this morning, perched on a dead branch at the top of a big old oak tree. It must have just arrived. The sound is subdued, but even from a distance I can see it lean forward for each 'cuck-oo' and get a sense of the effort it is putting in.

That slow, simple sound creates a nostalgic, relaxed feeling that's so evocative of the English spring and early summer. 🔊 4.17

I appreciate how lucky I am to hear it locally. The numbers arriving in England have declined massively over the last few years. When I give talks to Women's Institutes I'm often told that they never hear one near their home village anymore.

The cuckoo's shape, speed of flight and barred breast feathers make it look like a bird of prey, but it feeds exclusively on insects. They lay their eggs in the nests of much smaller birds, which end up rearing a huge alien chick instead of their own offspring. This behaviour has given cuckoos a dubious reputation. They perch with their wings at a rakish angle forward of their bodies, and if you're close enough you can hear them making short, rascally chuckles as they fly. But the soundscape of the spring countryside would be much poorer without them.

In the evening I walk past Crossway Hands Farm to the edge of Southwick Forest. I watch a hare ambling along the track, then carry on towards some oaks where tawny owls are tuning up in the dusk. After a while I can hear the birdsong behind me getting louder and go back to investigate.

A nightingale is singing there.

It is as if the everyday avian orchestra has simply been going through its routine paces and now the soloist has suddenly walked onstage and started playing. All the others are forced to raise their volume and standard of musicianship. The nightingale's tone is unmistakable: full, liquid and bubbling. It sings for just a few minutes then stops. All the other birds calm down too.

The nightingale carries on 'growling', making sounds like a thumbnail dragged across a comb that help mark its territory. That might be directed at other birds but could also be aimed at me. I decide it is time to leave. The forest is incredibly quiet as I walk happily back in the dark to the sound of my own footsteps. There is a soft glow from the slimmest of thin new moons. The year's first cuckoo and nightingale! What a relief and delight it is to have heard them both on the same day!

16 APRIL: I've been thinking about how birds get their English names. Some are onomatopoeic and describe the sound they make, as in cuckoo, curlew and chiffchaff. Others might be associated with a particular habitat like the reed and willow warblers. Colour comes into it too, as in goldfinch and blackbird. Some are named after the people who first described them: Cetti's warbler and Montagu's harrier. And some may be named after what they do: oystercatcher, woodpecker and the kingfisher itself.

In other languages the naming may be more elliptical. In many European countries kingfishers have names that translate as 'icebird', because it's often seen migrating in winter to find waters that are free of ice. In France it's called 'martin-pêcheur' after a legend that the species brings calm weather in November, which is around the time of St Martin's Day.

18 APRIL: I want to find out how many nightingales have arrived locally. The best way to do that is to be up before dawn when they sing to mark their territories. I set the alarm for 4.30am but wake an hour earlier, too excited to get back to sleep. I get up and load my recording gear into the car, then set off for the woods. There are no nightingales singing at Glapthorn, or in other stopping places around Southwick, but when I park near Crossway Hands I can

hear the distant crackle of a nightingale's song against the stillness of the night.

I walk up the steep road past the farm with my moon shadow leading the way. At the top of the hill I think I can hear a low rhythmic thumping that might be an outdoor rave going on in the distance. Many times I've recorded at night and on early spring mornings and picked up the beat of giant bass bins in fields miles away. But it slows and quietens when I stop to listen. It's my own heart thumping in the hush. I carry on along the track that skirts the forest, aware of the sound and weight of my footsteps in the chilly air.

Another nightingale is singing on its own, deep in the forest to my right. There's the beginning of a glow on the eastern horizon. I'm about to witness an extraordinary natural phenomenon that happens every day across the world and involves many species of birds: the dawn chorus.

Scientists are still working out why it happens. Singing is part of natural selection. Birds do it to guard their territory and attract a mate. Their song carries better at dawn when the air is cool and still. It's also a time when prey may be hard to spot. It makes sense to sing rather than feed. It's also a reminder to rivals that the bird has lived through the night. And it just might be a simple celebration of a new day, which is how humans are inclined to hear it.

When I get to the end of the track there are two nightingales singing. Then there's an explosive call from a pheasant. A thin glimmer of sound starts to rise from the fields all around: skylarks. A robin sings a little ribbon of song. Another answers. Song thrushes and blackbirds join in. They seem hesitant at first, but then there's a point where everything seems to start calling at once. Chaffinches and great tits, wrens and blackcaps, cuckoos and tawny owls all sound like they are shouting to be heard. It's like a rush hour for birds, a period of frantic activity that fades gradually as they finish making their point and start to feed. ◀ 4.18

While walking in the dark, I was taken into myself. Now I've been taken out again. The landscape glows in the early-morning light and my soul does too. The dawn chorus is an extraordinary performance, and it happens every day in spring. I can't believe that I lived so much of my life without properly appreciating it.

21 APRIL: There's a newly arrived reed warbler singing in the meadows. Of all the migrant birds its percussive, syncopated song sounds like it's come from Africa. It popped out of the reed bed at one point, and I marvelled that such a tiny thing could make such stirring sound. ◀ 4.19

Even more remarkable is that it can end its breeding season raising a cuckoo chick many times larger than itself. Reed warbler nests are a prime target for female cuckoos to lay their eggs.

On the way back I spot a kingfisher perching quietly on a willow branch. It isn't looking into the water and doesn't dive after a fish for many minutes. It may be keeping a lookout, but I've not heard much calling recently. Perhaps its neighbours are focussed on their own nests and territories. This seems to be a much calmer period for the local kingfishers.

22 APRIL: There is an amazing range of sounds in Southwick Forest tonight. A honk like a tugboat from a passing raven makes me jump and seems to set the trees quivering. Gilbert White

described something similar: "Ravens, beside their loud croak, can exert a deep and solemn note that makes the woods to echo."

There are wobbly tawny owls and screeching barn owls, followed by the hoarse barks of a muntjac deer. Then a lone grasshopper warbler starts reeling, quietly singing in the darkened scrub. The volume comes and goes as the bird slowly turns its head from side to side. It actually sounds like a grasshopper, and comes from a genus named *Locustella* because of their insect-like calls. White himself had great difficulty in convincing his companions that they were listening to a bird. ◀◊ 4.20

The range of different sounds that birds make is extraordinary.

23 APRIL: Every year on St George's Day I walk up to listen to birdsong in the forest above Southwick village. Often there's a nightingale singing there, and I've never failed to hear a cuckoo. I lived in the valley below the forest at Southwick Hall for seven years in the 1980s. I rented a flat in a part of the building that dated from Tudor times and made instruments in the original fourteenth-century tower. It was an extraordinary place to live, and hearing cuckoos is part of my abiding memory of the place.

There's a workshop there in the old stable block. Over the years the estate staff have pencilled graffiti on the walls. Much of it is the addresses and telephone numbers of local farmers and agricultural businesses, and the workings out of sums to do with seeds and produce. But there are also dates when they heard the first cuckoo of spring. In 1927 it was 17 April. In 1938, the 21st. In 1950 it was the 18th. They're all in different handwriting. Some are firmer and more confident than others, but they all wanted to mark and share the joy of a simple and universal marker of spring.

25 APRIL: I get up early and stand looking down on the meadows from the bridge. The gentlest of breezes is blowing the early-morning mist across the river from right to left. The willow that marks the start of my river walk keeps disappearing and reappearing as thicker clouds move through. Only the tops of the trees in the wood are showing above it.

I come down from the bridge and walk towards the kingfisher nest. It is chilly, and the only other walker is hurrying along with hunched shoulders. There is no activity at the kingfisher nest, but there may just be a lull between deliveries of fish to the chicks. Judging by the time that I thought they started sitting on the eggs, I'd expect the chicks to start appearing in about a week or so.

26 APRIL: At around 11am I go and see whether nightingales are singing during the day in the forest past Boars Hill Farm. There is one calling as I arrive. While I am standing on the track a man who looks dressed for the countryside appears in the distance. As he walks towards me, I am slightly nervous of a confrontation, even though I am on a public bridleway. The local shooters have been known to be unwelcoming towards walkers. But as he gets nearer I notice that he has a bird ringer's badge on his jumper. Hanging round his neck are four cloth bags. I can see the gentle movements of live birds through the fabric.

"What a lovely sound," I say, nodding towards the nightingale, which is singing deep in some scrub. "You'll be lucky to see one though!" he replies. I can only agree. They're notoriously shy and I've only got a single photo of one in all the years I've been trying. We get talking and walk slowly along the track towards a clearing where a net is stretched between two wooden posts. It is like a long badminton net that reaches down to the ground and has billowing pockets designed to catch birds without harming them.

The man explains that he is researching how many nightingales there are in the forest, and whether they have success in hatching and fledging chicks. I've heard four nightingales singing there so far this year. He has heard a couple more. Some years they get into double figures, which is a lot these days for a bird near the northern limits of its range after flying all the way from Africa. There's no shortage of nightingales on the continent, but the numbers that make it to this side of the Channel are dwindling. The biggest strongholds are Kent and Sussex. A survey by the British Trust for Ornithology suggested that there were only 5,500 male nightingales singing in England during 2012. There could be a lot fewer now.

I'm attracted to nightingale song because of my musical interests and a fascination with sounds of all kinds. For me the experience of nightingales is mostly to do with the sounds and the emotions they evoke. But as the ringer and I talk it becomes clear that he's caught and ringed many of the actual birds I have listened to. He's handled them, felt their heartbeats and enjoyed a closeness I could never dream of. He caught the adults at the beginning of the season. At the end he will try to catch the juveniles too. He knows that the nightingale I was listening to earlier had produced at least three young last year because he had personally ringed them all.

To me that is breathtaking, something I would never have imagined. I've read that nightingales return to where they were born after flying thousands of miles to Africa and back. But the ringer knows that because he has only once caught a bird that had been originally ringed any distance away, and that was at Rutland

Water, just fifteen miles away. There was a spot at the top of the path from Southwick that had a singing nightingale every year until a couple of years ago. He'd ringed that very bird in 2011 and caught it in the same place annually for seven more years.

This was beginning to put a completely different spin on things I had tried to work out for myself. Now I understood that the loss of a singing nightingale could just be the result of a bird dying naturally of old age. And if that particular bird had always sung right through the night for the whole season it might never have paired up. There would be no young to follow in its wingbeats.

During our conversation a nightingale occasionally sings or growls from a thicket close by. The net is set up to catch him if he makes a dash across the clearing, but when he finally appears, he flies right round it and disappears into bushes on the far side. Birds caught earlier in a net further down the track included three grasshopper warblers, which are also considered to be rare. A couple of times the man has even caught kingfishers here, even though it is a long way from a proper running stream. By now there are two nightingales singing, one on either side of us. A turtle dove starts its soft purring call from the undergrowth nearby. It was once a common sound in this landscape, but now it's a rarity after a steep decline in numbers. ◀◗ 4.21

The ringer has been here since 6am. It is now midday. Nearly time to call it quits. What a wonderful way to spend time in the woods at the very best time of year.

28 APRIL: In *Song of Myself, 31*, Walt Whitman wrote: "I believe a leaf of grass is no less than the journey work of the stars." I don't feel much connection with the stars. But I do with the earth around

my feet and all the small things that loom up when I get down on all fours and sniff the ground. I feel a strong urge to do that this morning when I go to Southwick Wood to see the bluebells. The main trigger is the honeyed scent of the flowers themselves, and the fascinating shapes of some pink and purple orchids scattered among them. I love looking at the watery waves of bluebells stretching away through the trees, but also need to get much closer.

I kneel on the path and start by looking at the beautifully formed heads of the flowers themselves. Then I gradually work my way down their stalks and leaves to the ground beneath them. There is an earthy smell of moss, twigs and dry brown oak leaves. There are a few confetti petals from a wild cherry, then a snail shell and a fluffy white feather. I rummage in the leaf mould and discover a stash of last year's acorn holders. Their rough wooden cups might have been the bowls of tiny clay pipes. As I move a twig to one side a single blue beetle's wing unexpectedly shines in the light from the sky above.

A chaffinch calls from a branch. A speckled wood butterfly flies close enough to touch. I stand up and walk back along the path, enjoying the fresh green leaves and the yellow celandines, and the white stitchwort and wood anemones set against the deep blue backdrop. I stop to catch the spicy spring scent of a flowering hawthorn and marvel at the simple beauty of the petals and the purple tips on their stamens.

The bare-earth path offers up one more gift before I leave the wood: a brown and cream-streaked owl feather. It seems part feather, part leaf. The pattern is so subtle that it looks like the brown colours have blotted into the white, and the tawny parts have been dabbed on towards the edge. I walk along, stroking it gently back into its perfect shape. As I glance at the bluebells either side of the path, I see them as tiny musical bells. An old nursery song starts playing in my head: "Rings on her fingers and bells on her toes, and she shall have music wherever she goes…"

MAY

1 MAY: It's May Day. I leave the house at 3am, stop by the water tower at the top of Southwick Hill, and listen in the darkened silence. To my joy there's the faint but unmistakable sound of a nightingale singing in Short Wood. It wasn't there two weeks ago, but now it's loud and clear. I push through the footpath gate and walk along the moonlit track towards the trees. A tawny owl hoots across the moonlit fields from a hedgerow near Glapthorn.

After a few minutes I'm at the wood. The singing's been getting steadily louder as I get closer, but once I'm in among the trees it's even more vibrant and compelling. A nightingale calling in the stillness of the night reaches up and out into the darkness, creating a cathedral of sound. I'm a pilgrim stumbling through a darkened wood, a penitent tripping over tree roots in a stagger towards a shrine. At last I'm standing close by as it calls from a thicket by the path. The sound's so intense that I need to move several yards back down the path to protect my ears. As the sky lightens, other birds start to join in. A cuckoo calls from across the valley.

The nightingale starts to move around a small patch of territory and sings for a few minutes from a branch above my head. I can just glimpse it against the brightening sky. Its head is tilted back, throat vibrating, flexing its whole body in the pursuit of sound. It makes me think of John Clare's poem *The Nightingale's Nest*. Other poets use nightingales as symbolic devices, but he's keen to share the real bird with the reader. He beckons you in like a nineteenth-century David Attenborough and invites you to join him while he crawls into a thicket. Then he describes how he nestles down and:

> *…watched her while she sung – and her renown*
> *Hath made me marvel that so famed a bird*
> *Should have no better dress than russet brown.*
> *Her wings would tremble in her ecstasy*
> *And feathers stand on end as 'twere with joy*
> *And mouth wide open to release her heart*
> *Of its out-sobbing songs…*

Later in the poem he finds the nest itself:

> *The nest is made an hermit's mossy cell.*
> *Snug lies her curious eggs, in number five,*
> *Of deadened green or rather olive brown*

The nightingale I'm watching moves on and stops singing. I walk back to the entrance of the wood and then return along the path. Two yellowhammers fly towards each other and arc upwards with their breasts almost touching. A fox trots across the road as I drive back down the hill. I step back into the house, humbled by what I've seen and heard, and aware of how insulated we've become from these great natural celebrations.

2 MAY: Gerald Manley Hopkins opened his poem *Spring* by writing that: "Nothing is so beautiful as spring/When weeds, in wheels, shoot long and lovely and lush".

This is a giddy time in the woods and meadows. The leaves are coming out in every shade of green. I'm up early and out late, getting my fill of bluebells and birdsong, trying to keep up with it all. If I miss a walk for a few days it's like coming back to a different place. Nettles that were once around my ankles are beyond my knees, and the cow parsley is nearly up to my chest. The salt–spice scent of May blossom hangs in the air. I notice new plants almost daily. I occupy the shrinking dappled space in the woods between the undergrowth and the canopy.

3 MAY: The river has been getting busier over the last few weeks. It started with canoes and paddleboards. Now there's the occasional chug of a narrowboat. An online search of boats on UK waterways comes up with nearly four hundred craft named *Kingfisher*. I've seen one of them go by with beautifully painted orange and blue livery.

Another popular name is *Halcyon Days*. Halcyon is the Latin word for kingfisher, and the bird is linked with settled weather in Ancient Greek mythology. It's a phrase that conjures up a nostalgic picture of endless happy summer days, often in a person's youth.

4 MAY: I release my song *Kingfisher Blue* on the internet today. 'Released' seems an apt word to use. I am freeing a creation that's been loved and nurtured into life. The next stage is to set it free to take its own chances in the world.

I'm also delighted to say that the kingfisher chicks appear to have hatched. From a distance I can see and hear a lot of activity around the nest this morning. At least one of the adults flies towards it with a fish laid longways in its beak with the head showing, which is the way they present food to hungry chicks.

In their books, Eastman and Boag describe how the new chicks have blind eyes, bare pink skin and large heads. They gradually grow soft spines that evolve into coloured feathers. They'll stay in the nest for around twenty-five days, and by then the feathers will have fully developed. When the young leave the nest, they will need to develop fishing and flying skills very quickly and a full set of feathers is vital to achieve that.

As I pass Cotterstock lock I notice a blue tit flying into an opening in a lifebelt mounted on a post. I watch for ten minutes as it bobs in and out. The ingenuity birds show in finding suitable nest sites is boundless. Let's just hope that no swimmer gets into difficulties and needs to be thrown a lifeline.

5 MAY: When I was a child, the occasional walk together was one of the few points of contact with my father. I've walked almost every day since, sometimes for many hours. The combination of rhythmic, repetitive movements while moving through the landscape has become like a drug. It's something I miss when it's not there. Walking is the first and most basic form of transport. It fits in with the human scale and opens all your senses to the experience.

It can be a time to let thoughts fly, though that's not always a good thing. Sometimes I get to the end of a walk and think: "Why did I stay inside my head all the way round?" I may have been plodding along with my eyes down and not noticed anything around me, or even felt the tread of a single step. But at other times it's as if I'm following a free-flowing current that glides effortlessly along. My mind is liberated, and new forms of words and music can start to emerge. I carry a notebook and sometimes stop to write things down. But if an idea has real merit then the memory of it will still be there when I get home.

There are many different words to describe a walk: trek, roam, ramble, drift, amble and meander. Another lovely word is saunter. It means to stroll in a relaxed and open way. A walk can be a quiet time, allowing sounds to seep in from outside that might not normally be noticed. If you're really listening, the landscape has a lot to say.

I need to walk every day, and morning's always best. The American writer and naturalist Henry David Thoreau wrote that: "An early-morning walk is a blessing for the whole day". It's a chance to engage with the wonders of each new day, and to exercise the physical and mental muscles needed to appreciate it. Regular walking is like playing scales on an instrument. It's a repetitive run through of all the most basic elements of experience which makes it easier to pick out unusual sights and sounds when they happen.

Aside from my regular walks I also love to truly explore new places and even get lost. It taps into feelings I had as a child when I first broke out on my own. I only went a mile or two to the nearest town, but it could just as well have been a walk across the world. The human journey started in just the same way: short walks from home that became ever longer and more adventurous.

7 MAY: I find cuckoo calls magnetic. It's impossible not to stop and listen. They command attention. The birds themselves can be hard to spot, but it's always worth looking at the very top of a

tree. They often preach from the highest pulpit they can find. The calls are at a lower pitch than most birdsong, slow and predictable. After passages of steady calling there can be an erratic pause long enough to think it's given up. Then it starts again. As dark falls it can suddenly surprise you with an unexpected burst.

I once stood close to a cuckoo that was calling while another was answering from a few hundred yards away. At first I thought the distant one was an echo, but then it gradually went out of phase with the original until there were clearly two. The nearer one then stopped and took off, calling as it flew. Straight away there was the ecstatic bubbling trill of a female cuckoo in the undergrowth. To me it's one of the strangest sounds in the English countryside. I only once managed to record it, when I was listening to two nightingales and the cuckoo trilled right in front of me. ◀◈ 5.22

I only hear that sound a few times each year. Scientists think that they mimic the sound of a sparrowhawk to frighten reed warblers and dunnocks from their nests. Then they sneak in and lay one of their own eggs.

It starts to rain so I shelter under an oak tree, listening as the drops trickle through the leaves to the forest floor. A distant cuckoo begins to count down the dusk. The air fills with the scent of honeysuckle, pine and camomile.

9 MAY: After the overnight rain the meadows are full of warm and fragrant breezes. I can almost see and hear the grass grow. The river has swollen, and I can't help worrying about the kingfishers trying to provide for their new chicks. I go to check, but I needn't have bothered. A goose's nest has been swamped just upstream, but the kingfisher's nest hole is high enough above the river not to

be flooded. Even so, the water is faster and muddier, which makes fishing more difficult.

Three things reassure me though. As I pass by, workmen are opening up the lock to let the floodwater through. That means there'll be less flow over the weirs upstream of the nest. I also guess correctly that the mill race at Cotterstock will be slower, calmer and better for fishing. I am duly rewarded with the sight of a kingfisher perched there just above the water, half-hidden by a tangle of twigs and branches. And lastly, as I return past the nest, a bird flies off in a great wheeling arc and carries on along the brook that comes in from Glapthorn. A few minutes later it comes back with a fish and heads towards its nest. They know where to find shallower or stiller waters.

12 MAY: There's an oak tree in Southwick Forest that's several centuries old. I've been visiting it for nearly forty years to check that it's still standing and to sit on its exposed roots. It's become a good friend and counsellor, particularly when I'm worried about friends and family. It helps give a sense of perspective.

I go there towards evening, plunging off the forest road into the undergrowth, threading along the deer tracks between the saplings and brambles. I'm never quite sure where it is, but then its gnarled and broken old trunk suddenly looms up like an exclamation mark among the greenery. It is broad at the base and tapers towards the top like a wigwam tent.

When I first visited, I thought it was still alive, but the few green leaves I saw near its crown may have belonged to a hawthorn tree growing within it. What's left of the trunk is about fifteen feet tall. It's shattered, and large parts have hollowed out and fallen away so you can see through wide cracks to the other side. In some ways it's like the skeleton of a ruined building. Holes left in the trunk when the boughs fell could be roundels in a coarse stone wall. It's also a fine natural sculpture, curved and smooth and free of bark. The tough grey timber contrasts with the rotting brown inner wood and with the bright living greens and yellows of the moss and lichen. Like many ancient things it's unsettling to look at but oddly reassuring too, like the galled and fissured carcass of a whale or dinosaur.

Young sycamore trees grow close to it now, but a wider circle of mature oaks marks the full extent of its former canopy. A fallen bough stretches out a dozen paces away from the trunk. It undulates along the ground like a boat's keel then rears up into the prow of a Viking ship. Other timbers lie about, split along their length but still strong. They're like half-finished struts and spars in an abandoned boatyard. Ferns shoot up from the compost gathered in their larger cracks and openings.

I go back to the trunk and walk carefully round it. It must be at least twenty-five feet in circumference. During the tree's prime the forest would have been an important and productive place, and many people will have made their living from it. Wild boar and domestic pigs may have foraged here for acorns. Today it's a home for badgers. Sett entrances have been dug down into the roots on every side. Straw and earth litter the paths down into them. The sharp tang of urine mingles with a faint smell of woodsmoke drifting from a bonfire across the valley. I imagine the badgers crouched in the dark, listening to my footsteps overhead.

I sit back down on a tree root and listen. A cuckoo and a nightingale are calling, and a buzzard wheels and mews overhead.

A jay chatters, and a sudden breeze sends the leaves whispering. It's an enchanted place, and I know I'm lucky to be here. The tree has stood through storm and drought. It's heard the menacing drone of wartime bombers and the gentle echoes of church bells marking the births and deaths of countless generations in the villages close by. It gives me a sense of scale and grounding like nothing else I know.

14 MAY: At about this time of year in 1812, John Clare walked from his home village of Helpston to Peterborough. He was eighteen, and he went there to sign up and train with the Northamptonshire Militia. The government was concerned that Napoleon Bonaparte might be preparing to cross the Channel and invade. Young men could voluntarily join up for a bounty, or wait for conscription and get nothing. Clare opted to take the bounty. He and his colleagues were marched from Peterborough to Oundle for basic training in the meadows and fields nearby.

There were more than a thousand young men altogether. It must have been an extraordinary atmosphere in what was then little more than a village. Clare stayed at the Rose and Crown pub, which still stands in the old part of the town near St Peter's church. He was under five feet tall so was put in a platoon for undersized men. As a farm labourer he would have been tough and strong, but he wasn't considered to be the most focussed and cooperative of men. His head was already "full of poesy". A sergeant picked on him and he fought back. He was lucky to get off with just extra guard duties.

Clare had shown a remarkable empathy for nature since boyhood, and it's fascinating to think about what he may have seen and heard during his stay in Oundle. Nightingales would have been much more common then, singing in the thickets at the edge of town or even in domestic gardens. The valley would have been swarming with birds and wildlife. He was also an accomplished fiddler and knew all the songs that would have been sung in pubs or by campfires. He was part of a big group of young men away from their homes, and there would have been plenty of high spirits. It's not hard to imagine him singing, or even playing if he had access to an instrument.

Clare was called back to Oundle the following year for more training, but fears of invasion diminished and he never actually had to serve. By now he was beginning to write in a more organised way. In 1814 he made contact with a bookseller in Stamford that led to his first book being published in 1820. He would become famous as 'The Peasant Poet', and his intimate knowledge of the wildlife and countryside around his home led him to create some of the finest nature poems in the English language.

15 MAY: The dawn chorus is justly celebrated, but I love the evening chorus just as much. There's a golden twenty minutes or so when the sounds of the day swell and fall away. Tonight I'm in Southwick Forest, listening to a cuckoo, nightingales, tawny owls, the gentle croon of a turtle dove and the thin fizzle of a grasshopper warbler from a nearby clearing. I'm lucky to even hear all those sounds at the same time, but magically this is on a calm evening with my microphones pointed in the right direction and the recorder switched on. After a few minutes I listen back to what I heard, and it's beautifully clear and atmospheric. I'd put it in the top half dozen of the most evocative wildlife sound recordings I've ever done. ◀◉ 5.23

On my way back along the track a muntjac deer starts to bark from deep in the forest. Muntjacs aren't a native species, but were brought from China to Woburn Park in Bedfordshire in the nineteenth century and have since become widespread. Even though they're an inoffensive animal the size of a large dog, their sound can be frightening to anyone who doesn't know what it is. I stop to listen, and the dogs from a distant farm start barking in competition with it. 🔊 5.24

There's a brief lull, which is broken by the distant creepy screech of a barn owl. If that had been closer and louder it genuinely would have been a sound to freeze the blood. 🔊 5.25

18 MAY: As a child and adolescent I had no idea what trespass meant. I would look up local maps and find an interesting patch of water to explore: a pond, lake or river surrounded by woodland. Then I'd go out through the front door of our forces' married quarters, effectively a three-bedroomed council house, and cycle there. It wasn't till I got to university that I mixed and became friends with people who came from a landed background. I was walking in the countryside with one and suggested we hop over a low wooden fence to have a closer look at a beautiful old oak tree. "But that land belongs to somebody!" was the reply. I looked round and there wasn't a building for miles. I was puzzled as to why he thought that made any difference. Now I can appreciate the arguments about protecting private property. But I'm still puzzled about how we've ended up in a situation where rich individuals can legally keep the rest of us out of beautiful places that are often miles from their homes. Much of the time it's just so that gamebirds can be raised and shot for profit.

John Clare knew all about trespass. The Enclosures arrived in Helpston between the time of his adolescence and his mid-twenties. Common land and landmarks that had been used by the villagers for centuries were fenced off. In his sonnet *Trespass* he wrote:

> *I dreaded walking where there was no path*
> *And pressed with cautious tread the meadow swath*
> *And always turned to look with wary eye*
> *And always feared the owner coming by*

If you'd met a gamekeeper on private land two hundred years ago, and he thought you were up to no good, then the result could be a severe beating. If you resisted, you would be up before the magistrate. He was likely to be a landowner, and it was perfectly possible to be punished by transportation to Australia. In a lifetime of what I like to call 'benign trespass' I've had the occasional telling-off. I felt like a child back in school, being dressed down by the headteacher after being caught out of bounds. But that's hardly the same thing.

I was on the public footpath through the forest last night and heard some nightingales calling a hundred yards or so into the woods away from the path. I took off into a dense patch of woodland until I found a spot between two singers with a third a little further off. I'd rather not have to leave the footpath, and always feel relieved when I get back on it. But in some ways it's good to be nervous and wary. It feels more in keeping with nature as a whole and the creatures you're observing.

After a while I got a feeling I was being watched. I turned round and scanned the young ash trees and dense green undergrowth in front of me. I saw nothing unusual, but something must have looked out of place and my eyes were drawn back to a small rounded shape on a branch about twenty-five feet away. A tawny owlet sleepily met my gaze, its eyes barely open. It resembled a fuzzy grey felt toy with a beak attached.

It turned its head every now and lifted its stubby wings as if to relax them. Blackbirds started to call with a rhythmic clucking all around me. In the woods that often means that an adult owl is about. I got a brief glimpse of a tawny owl peering down from the crook of a tree to my left before it took off and flew across to the right. Then it settled low in a tree a few yards behind me and, as I turned round, its partner arrived too.

I didn't want to disturb the family, and they were alarmingly close. It's not unknown for tawny owls to attack an intruder, and trailblazing wildlife photographer Eric Hosking actually lost an eye to one in the 1940s. It was time to leave. I'd become involved in a family psychodrama, which wasn't my original intention. This really did feel like trespassing.

19 MAY: On this day in 1924 the BBC made its first live outside radio broadcast. Radio was in its infancy and the corporation had only started transmitting two years before. The nerves and anticipation must have been palpable when vanloads of equipment arrived at a house in a Surrey woodland. The engineers began to set up in microphones in the garden. The strange and wonderful sound they were hoping to capture and transmit later that evening was a woman playing a cello while wild nightingales sang from nearby thickets.

The player was Beatrice Harrison, who at the age of thirty-one was the most celebrated British cellist of her time. During a broadcast performance of Elgar's Cello Concerto she had the idea of persuading the BBC to transmit the nightingales that started to sing when she practised in her garden. It was an extraordinary suggestion that required a great leap of faith from Lord Reith, the Director General. He was being asked to set up an expensive live broadcast that was completely reliant on unpredictable wild birds. He agreed, and a million people heard the unique combination of sounds which started at 10.45pm and was broadcast for fifteen minutes.

It's recently been suggested that the nightingales had been disturbed by the technicians and didn't actually sing, and that a human impressionist had been called in to deputise for them. If that's true it still doesn't detract from the wonderful and eccentric idea behind the whole event. There was a tremendous reaction from the public and the cello and nightingales became an annual fixture in the BBC calendar. After Harrison moved house twelve years later the BBC carried on broadcasting nightingales singing on their own until 1943. In that year British bombers were heard in the sky as they set off for Germany. That could have been useful information for the enemy so the transmission was abandoned. Luckily for history, a stirring and poignant recording was made of a single nightingale singing against the throbbing drone of the massed ranks of aircraft passing overhead.

Nightingales often start to sing in reaction to loud noises. I've been in woods many times at night when the sound of a passing aircraft set them off. The 'duet' between nightingales and bombers is very likely to have happened around Oundle during wartime, as aircraft flew to Germany from a United States Airforce base in nearby Polebrook. One of the airmen based there was the Hollywood actor Clark Gable. He was involved in making recruitment films but also flew on risky bombing raids to Germany. In his free time he was a regular visitor to the Talbot Hotel in Oundle.

Another famous American who visited the area was the dance band leader Glenn Miller. His group played for the troops in a hangar at King's Cliffe in October 1944. Sadly, it was his last 'airfield concert' before his plane went missing on a flight across the channel.

20 MAY: I'm looking across the millpond, and there's a small white shape moving just above the water in the branches on the far side. I guess that it's the tail feathers of a moorhen, but when I zoom in with my camera I'm surprised to see that it's a fish being shaken about by a male kingfisher. They kill their catches by thrashing their beak from side to side to beat the fish against their perch, which also breaks the bones to make swallowing easier. It can be a messy business, and there are fish scales smeared along either side of the branch.

It takes a long time as the prey is almost as big as the predator, but eventually the fish becomes subdued and floppy. The kingfisher sets off with it in the direction of its nest a few hundred yards away. I can't imagine how it can fit such a big fish lengthwise in its beak, but it manages it somehow. As it passes I can see it straining under the weight, flying slower and with more effort than usual.

The fish's size makes me wonder if it will be split into pieces for the chicks. But researchers with cameras inside nests have found that the fish are always swallowed whole. If the fish is oversized the birds wait till their stomach acids have dissolved the head end before finally getting the tail end down their throats.

The youngsters should be nearly full grown by now. They'll be calling constantly for food. The adults will need to fish all day to provide for them. Their strength and stamina are being tested. I'm impressed and moved by what I've just seen. I don't usually give wild birds and animals names, but I'm going to have to start calling this one 'Hercules'.

25 MAY: It's glorious when the sun comes out in the meadows this afternoon. The grasses and flowers have grown so much in the last two weeks, and the air is thick with scents of tobacco, cinnamon, pepper and home-baking. The long grasses are dotted with flowers. There are clovers and forget-me-nots lower down, buttercups and a few purple thistles higher up. A sea of cow parsley stretches the hundred yards from the river to the stream.

The insects are coming into their own. A cloud of blue demoiselles flutters up from a patch of nettles as I pass, and there are butterflies there too: orange-tips, brimstones, small tortoiseshells and an exquisite small copper. They flit and flutter then rest, apparently at random. 'Butterfly mind' is a perfect description of a brain that can't settle. In ancient Greek the word 'psyche' means both butterfly and soul. It's not hard to see the connection between the two. They're beautiful and alive with colour, but fragile and insubstantial at the same time.

As I walk back home there are kingfisher calls in the wood where the brook flows in from Glapthorn. A pair of adults flies briefly around each other above the river, blue wings alternating with orange-feathered breasts as they bank and part to head off in different directions. It looks like they are courting again, and they'll be preparing to get straight on with a second brood as soon as the current young have fledged. It's likely that some of the fish the male is catching will once again be fed to the female to build up her weight for egg laying.

27 MAY: For a change I decide to explore a different section of the river with my canoe. I put it into the water above Barnwell lock, right next to the park. I haven't got far downstream before I notice a hole in a small section of bare earth in the bank opposite. My first thought is that it might be a kingfisher's nest, but it's barely a foot above the surface of the water. As I paddle closer I can see that it is oozing guano, and am startled to hear the sound of chicks churring away deep inside. They're making a continuous sound that's more reminiscent of insects than birds. I paddle back upstream, and sit watching and listening from a distance. ◀) 5.26

After about twenty minutes a kingfisher arrives with a fish and perches briefly on a sycamore branch opposite the nest. Then it flies straight across the river into the hole. It comes out again almost immediately and makes two shallow dives into the water before taking off downriver. The dives are to clean itself after going into the nest, because the chicks defecate in the tunnel and the adults' feathers are bound to be contaminated while passing along it. The whole thing is wonderfully efficient and straightforward, and no time is wasted before the bird wheels away downstream to resume fishing.

Nest holes would normally be much higher above the water to guard against flooding, but this is actually a safe place. The lock and its side channels are used to regulate floodwaters, and boats travel very slowly along this stretch so there's less risk of their wake swamping the nest. It may have been pure luck, but the kingfishers who built it seem to have known what they were doing.

28 MAY: As I'm walking around Oundle this evening I go down a path between two stone buildings and hear a sound that makes me stop and smile. It's a chiming tinkle of beeps with no obvious rhythm. The overall impression is quiet, though some sounds are louder than others. Newcomers who move to this part of town are sometimes bewildered when they hear what sounds like the electronic cheeps of a smoke alarm when the battery's running out. It's actually made by midwife toads. ◀) 5.27 This is one of the few places in England where they live and breed.

The toads are an alien species in this environment, though they're common in mainland Europe. They're thought to have arrived in Bedford in 1906 with potted plants imported from France. A schoolboy called Robert Brocklehurst brought some to Oundle when he was visiting relatives. They've thrived ever since in the back gardens of an area little more than a hundred yards square. It's rare to see one because they're tiny and hide in crevices and cracks between flagstones, but they keep up a steady drone of calling through the nights of spring and summer.

29 MAY: It's around the time that the kingfisher chicks should be fledging and flying from the nest on the river near Cotterstock. I sit in my usual place upstream for an hour, but there's no sign of any kingfisher activity. Then a single kingfisher flies high overhead towards the wooded part of the river.

I move a couple of hundred yards upstream and sit on a pile of logs left behind when a fallen tree was cleared. I'm sitting higher now, looking down on the water and enjoying the shimmering greens and yellows of the trees reflected on the river's surface. A pair of small tortoiseshell butterflies settles on some thistles to my left. Suddenly a kingfisher flies right above my head from the meadow behind me then banks into the trees following the line of the brook. It could be my imagination, but I think I hear answering calls before it reaches the other side of the wood.

I walk to Cotterstock and cross to the other side of the river so I can go into the trees where the kingfisher has flown. There are some chiming sounds which could be youngsters, but I can't get a clear view of what's making them. I give up the search for now. Hopefully there will be more activity tomorrow.

30 MAY: When I arrive at the river this morning there are kingfishers flying into the near bank opposite Snipe Meadow. It's too overgrown to see much, so I hurry back to the bridge and walk along the road towards the path on the far side. I'm excited. It feels strange to be walking past people enjoying the busy tennis courts and rugby pitches. I even have a short conversation when a man stops digging his allotment to chat.

When I get to the river kingfishers are still flying towards the bank. Suddenly an adult bursts out, pursued by two chicks. The parent bird settles on a bare dead branch above the water holding a small silver fish in its beak. The youngsters flit around it, squabbling to get close. There's a constant flutter of blue wings and short, sharp calls. One reaches in to grab the fish then sits with it while the other two flash noisily off downriver. Then it vanishes too.

I sit on a fallen log and rub my eyes. So much had built up to this moment, and it all happened so quickly. I'm not sure what I'd seen was real. But it was. The vivid sounds and colours were all I'd hoped they would be. I practically skip along the path back home. According to the books, the parents and chicks will only be together for a few days before the adults drive them away so they can get on with the next brood. But at least I'd seen them together, and there's the chance of more to come.

31 MAY: I'm watching a kingfisher perching in the open on the far side of the river, near where I saw the family group yesterday. It's small but perfectly formed and is quietly looking down into the water. When I zoom in with the camera, I can see it's a chick rather than an adult. The breast feathers are a rusty-brown colour, and the legs and feet are dark. Both will become more orange as it gets older. The beak is slightly shorter, and there's a white spot at its pointed tip which evolved so that the parents could see it more clearly in the gloom of the nest.

The fledgling shows its inexperience when it tries to fish. Every now and then it dives into the water, but rather than arrow down at a sharp angle it belly flops and struggles to get clear of the surface to fly back to its perch. At least it's getting more practice than its sibling, who's hiding behind the long, thin willow leaves at the river's edge. It's calling for a parent to bring it ready-caught food. The meal's slow to arrive, and it'll happen less and less frequently as each day passes. The chicks must be forced to learn to fend for themselves. But before I go, I catch one more brief tableau of an adult feeding two chicks. They land on a branch that's barely protruding from the river, and I can see their mirror-image reflections dart and flicker on the water as they dance around each other in sudden swirls of orange and blue.

JUNE

1 JUNE: Spring is turning to summer. Pink and white dogroses have begun to appear among the shrubs by the bridge. Dawns are less noisy now, but the days are warming up. There's plenty of life and growth still to come. As I get to the meadows a gentle breeze ruffles through the silver-green grass. A cuckoo calls, and I pick out his shape high in an ash tree. He pauses to preen as a female lets out a warm, bubbling cry from the reeds beneath.

I spot the two kingfisher chicks straight away on the far bank, tiny toylike scraps of blue and orange in the green willows just above the water. One dives into the river with a faint splosh, then returns to a perch higher up and dives again. It does this several times, diving from different heights and angles. Each time it flies up I pray it'll have a fish in its beak, but it struggles to catch anything. At last, it lands back on a branch holding a thin silver slip of a minnow.

After that both birds move deeper into the overhanging twigs so I can't see them. I head for home then go back again in the evening, but this time I can't find them. It seems likely that they've moved on to other parts of the river. It feels like the end of a chapter, and I wish them luck. It's the beginning of a new one too. The parents will already be preparing for a second brood.

3 JUNE: I've been reading about a type of Chinese jewellery called Tian-Tsui, which was made with kingfisher feathers. They were painstakingly inlaid into elaborate metal hairpins and bridal caps, then lacquered to look like enamel. The oldest examples date from the Qin dynasty in the second century BC and they were a symbol of imperial and aristocratic status for over two thousand years.

After finding out that there are some pieces in the Pitt Rivers Museum in Oxford, I go to see them. Two institutions are housed in the same impressive Victorian building. The first is the University Museum, which deals with natural history. Bright daylight shines through the ornate glass roof as I walk around the beautifully designed displays of stuffed birds and animals.

After passing through the natural history collection, the entrance to the Pitt Rivers Museum leads into a darker and more mysterious place. It is based on a collection of handmade artefacts from different cultures collected by General Augustus Pitt Rivers in the nineteenth century. The exhibits include clothes, weapons, tools, musical instruments and objects used in religion and magic. They have the cluttered, serendipitous feel of an old curiosity shop.

I head upstairs to a gallery where feathered objects and ornaments are displayed in a long glass case. They include a fan made from eagle feathers, used by Native Americans for spreading purifying smoke. It reminds me of a grey heron's wing I picked up from a display table in the educational centre of a local country park. It seemed ridiculously light for such a big object, but the feathers trapped the air so efficiently it was surprisingly difficult to wave back and forth.

There are also musical instruments made from feathers and bird parts, including Colombian pan pipes created from the hollow quills of a condor, a Greek flute formed from an eagle's wing bone and an ingenious Scandinavian rattle made with puffin beaks. I try to imagine what they would sound like, both separately and as part of a band. There'd be a breathy, airy tone from the pipes and a percussive clacking from the rattle. Next to them are an arrow with a feathered shaft and a goose-quill pen. Both inventions had a huge influence on human history.

At the back of the case are two Tian-Tsui brooches. They look beautifully made but small, and the blue feathers don't show up well in the low light. I'm a bit disappointed. Luckily a passing researcher asks what I am looking for. She explains that there are better examples in the Ashmolean Museum, a short distance across town.

I leave the building and walk there through a mixture of narrow cobbled streets and busy modern thoroughfares. The Ashmolean was Britain's first public museum, founded in 1683. I pass through its grand pillared entrance into the marble halls inside. In one of the Chinese galleries I find two pieces of Tian-Tsui. They were made in the nineteenth century and the craftsmanship is exquisite. Each is based on a long hairpin and topped with a brooch about eight inches wide and four inches tall. They are made with gilt wire, precious stones, seed pearls and shaped metal forms into which kingfisher feathers are inlaid.

It is as if a cluster of iridescent butterflies has settled among the organic shapes of flowers and leaves. Some of the parts are set on thin wires so they would have jiggled when the wearer moved, varying the light and colour reflected by the feathers. Today we're used to all sorts of visual tricks, but their appearance is mesmerising. At the Chinese court the effect must have been dazzling. I gaze at them for a long time before I have to tear myself away and head back into the bustle and noise of the Oxford streets.

4 JUNE: I am back by the river this morning and see an electric flash of blue as a kingfisher flies past in the full light of the morning sun. It makes me think again about the jewellery I saw. That beauty was gained at great cost to the birds. There was a lucrative trade in their feathers. Many were imported into China from Cambodia, where the profits helped finance the building of the temples at Angkor Wat.

Wild birds have suffered in more recent times too. Before binoculars and photographs were available, the only way ornithologists could study them in detail was by capturing them and keeping them alive or killing them to stuff or preserve their skins. The destruction of birds spread far beyond the scientific community. In the Victorian period taxidermy and egg-collecting were fashionable. So was the use of feathers in ladies' hats. In 1886 the American ornithologist Frank Chapman watched women walking in an upmarket shopping district for two afternoons. In that time he identified the feathers of forty different species in their hats. It was estimated that up to five million birds were killed for their feathers in the US every year.

The hat trade in England threatened birds across the world, including little egrets and birds of paradise. Native birds like herons, owls and kingfishers weren't spared either. Small groups of women started to question what they called "murderous millinery". The British Ornithologists' Union only admitted men, so Emily Williamson started the Society for the Protection of Birds in 1889. The first all-women meetings were held at her home in Manchester.

The idea soon spread. A similar organisation was founded in Surrey by Etta Lemon and Eliza Phillips. The two groups amalgamated in 1891 and, after receiving the royal charter in 1904, were renamed the Royal Society for the Protection of Birds (RSPB). It took another seventeen years before the import of feathers to the UK was finally banned, but it meant that the RSPB had scored its first victory in the battle to conserve birds.

5 JUNE: There's been no more sign of the chicks on the stretch between Oundle and Cotterstock. I decide to walk down to Barnwell lock early in the morning to see if anything's happening near the nest I discovered while paddling my canoe. There's a strong sense of anticipation as I get to the bridge that overlooks that stretch of river. I lean against the chest-high concrete parapet and look across towards the lock and the stone mill building next to it. It would be hard to imagine a more picturesque scene of old rural England. Geese graze on the far bank, and there's the gentle rush of water through the mill race.

I watch and wait for half an hour. A pair of swans parade their eight cygnets across the grass and head towards the river. The adults' gait is comically exaggerated as they waddle slowly so the chicks can walk in a straight line between them. When they get to the bank most of the youngsters slide happily down the slope but two tumble head first into the water. Once in the river they're a picture of elegance and relaxation.

There's no coming and going from the kingfishers' nest, but I can hear bright bursts of calls from Barnwell Park off to the right. I walk there and head for the lake where the sounds have been coming from. Trees and undergrowth obscure the view to start with, but when I get to a gap I can see across to the far side. I concentrate on a section with a lot of bare willow branches that reach out over the water. It's about seventy yards away. There's a tiny patch of orange there, too small to see clearly with the naked eye. It looks like the breast feathers of a kingfisher. Another is perched a few feet away and I can hear the short chiming sounds of a chick calling for food. Then a turquoise shape streaks across the surface of the water towards them, and there's a brief and noisy exchange before it flies away again.

Another youngster arrives in the same tree and they sit quietly together. The parents have chosen a good place to fledge them. For most of the day the sun will be directly on the lake, and it's isolated from the main paths through the park. The water's calm and clear, and there are plenty of perches to fish from. Two of the chicks are sitting on a series of overlapping bare branches shaped like an elongated hoop laid on its side. As I'm watching an adult flies in and the other chick joins them. I get my camera out, and point and click, more in hope than anything else. They're a long way away and everything's happening very quickly.

They shoot off in all directions, so I look at the image and blow it up on the screen. I can't believe what I'm seeing. There are four kingfishers sitting in profile, equally spaced together on the hoop of branches. Three look to the left and the other's facing back towards them. There's a lovely shape and symmetry, and it could hardly be a better example of a 'crown of kingfishers'. The colours are glorious, the focus is sharp. To top it all, each of the birds has a glint of light reflecting off the eye. Birds' eyes don't always show up well against their feathers. The glint provides the surface flash of a diamond stone together with a hint of the warm and intelligent life within.

7 JUNE: It's arguable that no part of a river is more important than any other, but there's something fascinating about the source. That's where it's said to 'rise' and come to life, as if from nothing. I set out to find the furthest point of the Nene from the sea. The source there is fed by springs which flow from the limestone near an ancient fort at Arbury Hill, one of the highest points in Northamptonshire.

I park in Badby near the village green with its historic cottages built in rust-coloured ironstone. From the edge of the village I walk a public footpath that follows the Nene upstream through a series of meadows. At this point the river is only a few feet wide, flowing fast along a deep ditch well below the level of the surrounding fields. It looks peaceful now, but parts of the inner banks show signs of being scoured by floods. It's flanked by a wide range of trees, including fabulously twisted oaks, slender ashes, willows, hazels and sycamores.

Newly shorn sheep turn their dark faces and call towards me as I pass. In the next meadow the path skirts a waist-high crop of green barley with gold tips. At the end of a field is a tumbledown farm building with limestone walls patched up with old red bricks. Laid across them is a jumble of corrugated iron, greying timbers and a sprawling overcoat of dark, tangled ivy.

I push through a gate beyond it. There's a loud metallic click as it swings back against the latch. A green woodpecker rises from the grass with a jangling alarm call. Its yellow back and red head undulate up towards a single oak tree. To the right a shallow stream runs down into the valley from a spring near the top of the slope. Its course is clearly marked by the feathery green water horsetail plants growing round it. I walk up to the spring and kneel down. The water welling up is dark and cloudy. At first, I suspect it's polluted, but then realise it's coloured by ironstone in the rocks below. When I dip my fingers in it's cold and smells of rust.

The valley's getting narrower, and the grass slopes steeper. It feels more enclosed and ancient. The ground's boggy underfoot and the stream's disappeared under thick brambles. A sudden breeze masks the sound of flowing water. I imagine Iron Age warriors watching and waiting in the trees on the slopes above me. I've lost my place on the map and have a strange other-worldly feeling. I decide to turn back. I don't think I've found the original source, but I've got the feel of the terrain and kneel by a spring which must have been very close. It's enough for me.

10 JUNE: It is raining hard this morning. I brave a walk along the river but don't see a soul apart from a heron sitting in a tree. It is so huddled and hunched, head sunk way below its shoulders, that from a distance I think it is a wood pigeon. Later I stand below an ash tree while a cuckoo calls for a good five minutes. It is an unforgettable sound with the raindrops dripping through the canopy. At this time of year I've come to treasure every '*cuck*' and '*koo*', even with cold water trickling down the back of my neck.

At dusk, I walk through the rain-soaked trees by the river. The sounds of water dripping to the forest floor merge with the birds as they sing the day away. The air is a heady fug of warm, wet scents: low earthy tones of peat, tobacco and creosote, with occasional high notes of patchouli, mint and wintergreen.

11 JUNE: I've been thinking about why kingfishers are so attractive to look at. To start with, the shape of a perching kingfisher is pleasing. When it sits with its neck rested into the shoulders its

shape becomes rounded, relaxed and well proportioned, balancing the forward thrust of that long, sharp beak. It almost looks like it's pointing the way.

The blue and orange of the wing and breast feathers look pleasing together because they're on opposite sides of the colour wheel invented by Sir Isaac Newton in the seventeenth century. Artists and fashion designers talk about the two colours making one another 'pop' when they're placed next to each other. The contrast makes each seem brighter and more intense.

The exotic tropical colours of a kingfisher can seem out of place in the UK, especially when seen against the drab, camouflaged hues of winter. It's fair to ask two questions: why are they so brightly coloured in the first place, and how do they come to be here?

Bright feathers can be useful if a bird is trying to hide in foliage with similar colours, and males may evolve more colourful plumage to attract a mate. Certain colours may also signal to predators that they're not good to eat, which is a strategy used by some butterflies and moths with distinctive markings.

In a more northern landscape you might think that kingfishers would stand out too much from the green plants in summer and bare twigs in winter. But they can be difficult to spot. The division between blue and orange feathers makes their overall shape less visible. If they hide in the shade, the feathers don't reflect light. Their orange breasts can also look like an autumn leaf. It's possible that when a predator looks down on a flying kingfisher from above the bright stripe down its back disappears in the light reflected off the water.

Male and female kingfishers are equally colourful, so the explanation that the male evolves brighter plumage to get a mate doesn't seem to apply. But they spend large parts of the year apart, and it may be that both sexes evolved bright colours so they can see each other more easily in the period when they're breeding and rearing chicks.

Now to the second question: what are they doing here? Of the many different species of kingfishers in the world, most are thought to have originated in southeast Asia. The common kingfisher is still found there today, as well as across much of Europe and Asia. It's worth remembering that the climate has changed many times since birds evolved. Much of the UK once supported tropical plants and animals as well as birds. As the climate cooled, birds that lived on seeds or insects may not have survived or had to migrate. But there were enough small fish to support kingfishers throughout the year. So they thrived as a tropical species that was adaptable enough to live elsewhere even when conditions became very different.

12 JUNE: I go up to Southwick Forest at twilight. It's calm, heavy with the scent of honeysuckle, and there's still enough light to make out the white stripes of a badger crossing the path some way ahead. I stop to listen, and a hare comes trotting down the track. It comes to a halt just feet away. We meet each other's gaze for a few moments before it turns and ambles off. I hope I looked even half as intelligent to him as he did to me.

A cuckoo starts to call, then a nightingale starts reeling out bursts of song. Sometimes they finish singing by early June, but this year's slow spring looks to have extended the season. I'd be happy if they never stop, but when they do it's good news. It means the young have fledged.

I set up my recording gear, but have to wait to get a good recording. Man-made noises are mercifully few, but insects are buzzing so close to the microphones that they're a major distraction. They gradually calm down. The nightingale has gone quiet by now, but there's some lovely singing between blackbirds. I experience the pure joy of capturing the sounds and mood of the forest as it slips from day into night. 🔊 6.28

Later, on the walk back to the car, I think about what I have just been doing. I find birdsong fascinating and know that many others do too. But why is that? What are we listening to, and what are we hearing?

Humans have been surrounded by birdsong for millennia. We can't distinguish all the sounds birds can make. Many are too fast and high. But our hearing is well adapted to them. Being sensitive to the sounds of birds and animals will have been important for people living in forests. A change in the background voices, or an unusual silence, could mean that predators were near. We may find a well-balanced passage of birdsong beautiful and relaxing because it signalled to our ancestors that they were safe. For a modern city dweller surrounded by intrusive human noise birdsong may provide a flashback to a simpler and calmer environment.

It can give a powerful sense of place. When I perform in care homes for the elderly, I always play some of my birdsong recordings. They're very popular, and people sometimes tell me about times in their lives when birdsong was very important to them. Often they are women who remember being up at dawn when their children were very young.

We refer to bird*song* and the dawn *chorus*. Those italicised terms usually refer to human music. There are similarities. Many bird sounds are based on repeated rhythms and melodies, and the intervals and scales can sound familiar. They improvise and make the patterns more elaborate. The scientific argument may be that all they're doing is trying to mate and guard their territory, but humans use music to attract or upstage other people too.

Most birds stop singing at the end of the breeding season, but I've noticed that song thrushes often carry on into the autumn. Their song can even be more varied and tuneful at that time. Friends often send me recordings they've made on their phones at that time of year asking what they are. They're usually song thrushes. We have no way of knowing if birds actually enjoy singing in the same way as we might. But the motivation for human singing may not always be for enjoyment. It may be part of ritual or religious practice, or simply seen as an aspect of ordinary life that's no more important than any other.

Though birds are thought to sing only for their own species, there is a sense in which they're part of a chorus. Bernie Krause points out that birds fill in niches where the acoustic territory is unoccupied. Some sing low, some higher, and they'll evolve to make sounds that can be heard in the same way that groups of singers and instrumentalists do. Each instrument in an orchestra plays a different role in creating the overall sound.

16 JUNE: There's a good crop of buttercups in the meadows this year, and more damselflies than I've ever seen. While walking along, I'm looking out for little flashes of kingfisher blue on the far bank. The tiny shimmer of a banded demoiselle's blue wings close by can often cause false alarms, though welcome ones. I love the blur and fragility of the demoiselles, the moments of repose

followed by the jerky flight, and the way they dance around each other. There's a place by the bridge over the weir where they're drawn to the humidity. I can look straight down on them as they hover above the arrowhead plants.

The vegetation at the edge of the river has become magnificently tangled, growing taller and thicker by the day. I sit in the shade of a small tree with my feet dangling in the water. Some paddleboarders go by and congratulate me on finding such a cool spot to sit in. As the fish bask in the shallows, I realise that I've hit on a new way of being by the river. I'm a 'kingfisherman', sitting still and waiting for them to arrive. A few minutes later one flies by, heading upstream.

Eventually I decide to move on and walk through Cotterstock to the woods on the other side of the river. I find another cool spot by a natural flowerbed of purple loosestrife and white bindweed. I've brought my camera, so set it up on a tripod pointing along the river and leave it to take some video. It might make a good background for some music at some time in the future. Then I sit down and wait.

Suddenly I notice a flicker just above the water a couple of hundred yards away. It becomes bigger and clearer and faster as it approaches. It's a swan flying close to the water, and soon I can make out its pumping wings and long, outstretched neck and hear the loud, grating throb of its primary feathers. It passes within a few yards and heads off further downriver till the wingbeats fade and the river becomes quiet again. 🔊 6.29

I hardly dare to think that the camera's captured the swan's flight, and the dramatic rise and fall of its sound. But when I get home and watch the video on the laptop it's even more vivid than I'd hoped. If I'd been holding the camera, it would have been difficult to keep the onrushing swan in the frame. I'd have wobbled about and messed things up. But because it was fixed in one place it captured the whole sequence perfectly. It also sounds just as I remember. The rhythmic chuff of the wings is reminiscent of a steam train puffing by.

Then I notice that the downstroke of the swan's wings caused small pools of turbulence to form on the river's surface. They left a wake behind them, even though there was no direct contact. I do some research and find that the swan was taking advantage of what human pilots call 'ground effect'. It was making use of the extra lift gained by pushing the air against something more solid. It only works if the bird is within a wing's length of the water, which explains why it had been flying as if hugging the surface. It was combining strength, beauty and science in a way I would never have imagined.

18 JUNE: I saw some black hairstreaks, rare butterflies, at Glapthorn Cow Pastures this morning. I usually have the wood pretty much to myself, but as they only breed in a few places in Britain, all between Oxford and Peterborough, there were a couple of dozen people there who'd travelled from all over the country. Most were set on getting the best photograph they could of a butterfly settled on the brambles. That involved finding the best and most perfect specimens, and those that might be a bit tattered around the edges were described as "battered". I could see what they were getting at but felt sorry for the less perfect ones.

I thought of Pulitzer Prize-winning poet Robert Frost's description of butterflies as "flowers that fly and all but sing", and tried to imagine what sounds they might make if they had voices. In his love poem *I Like For You To Be Still*, the Chilean poet Pablo

Neruda used the extraordinary image of a "butterfly cooing like a dove". For me the sound it made would have to be shiny and ethereal, something like a Tibetan singing bowl.

21 JUNE: It's the morning of Solstice, astronomical midsummer. I imagine the crowds gathered at Stonehenge as I wake at 3.30am and go to meet the dawn on my own at Glapthorn. It's cold so I've dressed up well. There's thick white dew on the grass and a heavy hush. Then song thrushes begin to chorus from high in the trees, calling against a growing swell of sound from sheep and cattle in the fields beyond.

Robins and wrens join in closer to the ground, then blackbirds start their pure, sweet song. Their sounds gradually swell to reach right across the wood. Then rooks take off and fill the air with their harsh calls. There's a short rattle of a woodpecker and a single tawny hoot. The sky's lightening to the east and the sun swims into focus, splashing gold onto low boughs as it slowly pours over the rim of the wood. I feel its glow as steam lifts from piles of fallen branches and insects start to fly.

The sun rises higher, and a blackbird breaks off from singing to drop down from the trees and feed on a path. A few minutes later it flies back up and sings some more. A hare and a deer graze next to each other in a clearing, and I can smell the warming grass. The day's started and feeding has begun.

24 JUNE: When I stayed with my nan as a young child I'd run onto the footbridge over the railway near her home if I heard a steam train coming. Then I'd stand on tiptoe to watch as the engine puffed towards me, waiting for the delicious few seconds when clouds of

steam rose up and billowed around as it passed under the bridge and clattered on down the track.

My uncle Eric did the same when he was young, and he grew up to be a train driver. He started work as a steam-locomotive fireman during World War II when railways were targeted by German aircraft and blackout restrictions made train travel difficult and dangerous. Rail played a vital part in moving freight and troops, and if there was a signal that they might be attacked the crew had to stop immediately and direct the passengers to shelter on the track beneath the carriages.

After the war Eric graduated to become a driver and loved working as part of a two-man crew amid the visceral grime and noise of locomotives that pulsed and thrummed like living things. He delighted in cooking his breakfast bacon and eggs on a shovel heated by the firebox. After steam was phased out the job was never the same. He carried on driving diesel and electric trains between Bournemouth and London, sitting on his own in a cab wearing a clean, functional uniform. But he was counting the days to his retirement.

He was happiest in the little workshop at the end of his garden. I was fascinated by the smell of pinewood and lubricating oil as you went in, and the neatly arranged metal drills and drawers with brass handles. He always knew exactly where to look for tools and nails and screws. He'd made his own wooden boat there and used it to go fishing in Poole Harbour. I once went with him, and have wonderful memories of an early start on a bright, fresh day, wading through shallows with hard-ribbed sand beneath my bare feet then puttering past silver-beached islands full of pine trees and rhododendron bushes.

Today I am sitting by the river not far from home, listening to blackbirds. Their calls have become gentler since spring and they sing as if they don't have a care in the world, two or three voices winding round each other in the lazy haze of a summer afternoon. It makes me think of Edward Thomas's poem *Adlestrop*, where he describes hearing blackbirds when his train stops on a hot day at a remote country station.

I remember Adlestrop—
The name, because one afternoon
Of heat the express-train drew up there
Unwontedly. It was late June.

The steam hissed. Someone cleared his throat.
No one left and no one came
On the bare platform. What I saw
Was Adlestrop - only the name

And willows, willow-herb, and grass,
And meadowsweet, and haycocks dry,
No whit less still and lonely fair
Than the high cloudlets in the sky.

And for that minute a blackbird sang
Close by, and round him, mistier,
Farther and farther, all the birds
Of Oxfordshire and Gloucestershire.

Anyone who has travelled in a train with open windows (especially a steam train) might recall a stop at a quiet rural station, where the hypnotic drone of the engine on the tracks slowed and paused for a moment, and birdsong poured in the carriages. There'd be the smell of the dusty seats and the tang of warm soot. You might hazard a guess at how the name on the station platform was pronounced and wonder how this quiet place you'd never heard of came to be at the centre of other people's lives.

I love Thomas's poem for its atmosphere, images and sounds, and the way he uses the word 'mistier' to evoke the songs of birds stretching out into the smoky distance. It was inspired by a train journey he made in June 1914. World War I started a month later and the poet himself would be sent to France in the springtime of 1917. He was killed soon after.

Uncle Eric was born eight years later in 1925. Not long after retiring from the railway he became very ill with cancer and died in 1990, but I'll always remember him tinkering in his workshop or starting up the outboard motor on his boat in the harbour. And I imagine him as a younger man, shovelling coal into the firebox and pulling on the whistle chord, as the train he drives draws slowly away from a small country station and the blackbirds sing in the shimmering heat of an endless English summer.

26 JUNE: A bright sun and calm weather has brought out the butterflies. There are meadow browns, commas, small tortoiseshells, ringlets, common blues and marbled whites in the woods and meadows this morning. I find a solitary painted lady too, resting on the tousled head of a violet thistle. I crouch down low so I can see the light shining through the veins of her patterned wings. They are divided into panes of orange, black and white like an exquisite stained-glass window. There are hints of eyes and translucent marble in the colours too, and the wings are outlined with silvery light.

I move through the long grass on my knees till I turn my attention from butterflies to buttercups. The sun glows through them and blurs the edges of the petals. I let my eyes lose focus till I am aware of nothing but the warmth and tangle of light and life. Anyone walking by will have seen a man on his knees in a buttercup meadow, apparently lost in prayer. Which in a way isn't so far from the truth.

28 JUNE: There is a smallish, barred feather on the path through the wood this morning. I stoop to pick it up, thinking it might be from a bird of prey, but the yellowish green on one of the vanes shows it came from a green woodpecker. There are others scattered among tangles of grey down. From their light mottled appearance the bird may have been a recent fledgling.

There is no body, but there must have been quite a fight. At least one of the feathers belongs to a sparrowhawk. The woodpecker's long, pointed beak will have been a very dangerous weapon. They've been seen locked in long struggles with sparrowhawks which sometimes end with the hawk drowning its victim in a puddle.

I feel the need to lay the feathers out in a pattern to try to find some sort of sense and beauty in what had happened. It makes for a forlorn little collection nestling among the leaves and grass and twigs. My first thought is: "Damn you, sparrowhawk! There'll be one less woodpecker yaffling from the treetops next spring." But it might have been a draw. Both birds could still be alive and kicking, albeit with a few feathers missing from their plumage.

30 JUNE: I've seen and heard a few kingfishers fly by as I've walked to Cotterstock during the last few days, but there doesn't appear to

be any nesting going on. So I walk across town to see if the nest near Barnwell Park is being used for a second brood. Kingfishers often use the same nest hole twice, but not always. I stand behind the bridge parapet some distance away and watch. If they're sitting on a new clutch of eggs, they may only swap around every three hours or so. It could be a long wait.

After about twenty minutes a single kingfisher calls and flies past, but otherwise nothing happens. There are plenty of reasons to be cheerful though. The temperature's comfortable, and there's a moderate breeze. I've got a beautiful view of the watermill. It's four stories high with a dark wooden chute jutting out near the top. Next to it there's a magnificent weeping willow, its fronds waving gently in the breeze.

On the lawn on the far bank a green woodpecker forages for ants, pecking at the ground then making quick darting looks to the right and left to check it's safe. A pair of greenfinches lands nearby and feeds on the grass. A blackbird sings, then a mistle thrush. A late cuckoo calls against the sound of church bells from Wadenhoe. An hour passes, then two. There's still nothing happening at the nest.

A boat goes by towards the lock and there's a minor collision with the floating jetty. The couple on board have a short argument. At one point all the birds in the grass fly up as one into the trees. I instinctively look up for the angular profile of a sparrowhawk, but it's just a small mechanical drone whining overhead.

I've been waiting for three hours now, and the last hour's felt like hard work. I'm stiff, hungry and about to leave. Suddenly a kingfisher calls as it sweeps across in front of me and lands out of sight. After a few moments of quiet another bird bursts out of the nest and takes off downstream. Then the other bird flies in. I've been anticipating this moment for so long that it seems twice as large and colourful as I'd imagined.

If all this had happened a few moments after arriving I would still have enjoyed what I'd seen. But waiting made it much better. Why did I stay so long, to the point where most people would have given up? For a start I was curious, and keen to see with my own eyes whether the nest was being used. It was challenging to sit and focus for so long in one place, but also meditative. I felt a deep contact with nature, and with all those others who have sat and waited in the past. Parts of it were boring, even maddening. But it was also deeply satisfying.

JULY

*Fairies and angels   The old nest   Purple emperors   Wales
By the bridge   Young naturalist   Middle Level   Barn owl
Tiny butterflies   A kingfisher chick*

1 JULY: I was joking to a friend the other day that after a year watching kingfishers I'd be well equipped to start looking for fairies, or even angels. I felt there were similarities in that they might be all around us but most people have never seen one. I reckoned that the waiting, seeing and believing skills built up while birdwatching might come in useful.

Joking apart, it's interesting that fairies and angels are often depicted with wings. Like birds, they may appear and disappear in a mysterious way. Like kingfishers, they may also have a supernatural light and glow about them.

This morning I was reading about Carl Jung, the great Swiss psychoanalyst who devoted his life to unpicking the meanings of myth, magic and dreams. In his 1913 book *Memories, Dreams, and Reflections*, Jung talks about dreaming of a character called Philemon, a kind of imaginary spiritual mentor. In the dream Philemon appeared as an old man, with the horns of a bull and the wings of a kingfisher, flying across the sky. Jung later did a painting of the image in which Philemon resembles an angel. The dream gained even more significance for him when he unexpectedly found a dead kingfisher in his garden a few days later.

There's a sense of awe and celebration in the way poets have written about kingfishers. In *The Progress of Spring*, Tennyson describes them as "the secret splendour of the brooks". W.H. Davies declares that: "It was the rainbow gave thee birth". Gerard Manley Hopkins starts one of his most famous poems with the luminous first line: "As kingfishers catch fire, dragonflies draw flame". In his *Four Quartets*, T.S. Eliot uses the image of light on a kingfisher's wing as he reflects on special moments, the still points in a spinning world.

For a bird that flies so fast, it's interesting that kingfishers are often associated with calm. In Ancient Greek mythology Alcyone was transformed into a kingfisher after her husband Ceyx died in a shipwreck. When she made a nest on a beach it was nearly swamped by a storm. Her father Aeolus, god of the winds, calmed the waves to save it. Kingfishers became associated with periods of good weather, especially if they happened at an unusual time of year.

Another association with weather was the folk belief that if a dead kingfisher is hung up on a string indoors its beak will always point in the direction of the wind. Shakespeare refers to it in *King Lear*, where he writes of rebels turning: "their halcyon beaks/with every gale and vary of their masters".

The belief was proved wrong by Sir Thomas Browne, a seventeenth-century physician, scientist and author from Norwich. Using a new scientific approach championed by Francis Bacon, he researched and analysed the topic before setting up an experiment where two dead kingfishers were hung up side by side. Then he observed that their beaks ended up pointing in completely different directions.

3 JULY: Since the chicks left I've barely seen or heard kingfishers along the river towards Cotterstock. As there's been no activity near the old nest site it seems safe to take a closer look. The copse opposite is full of chest-high nettles, so I put on a thick jacket and trousers to avoid being stung. When I finally get a clear view of the bank I'm shocked. There's been a landslip, and there's no trace of the nest. The earth there had been dry and cracked, and I always worried that the tunnel might collapse on itself. Now the whole section of the bank has crumbled away and fallen into the water. If the kingfishers are planning a second brood, they must have built a new nest elsewhere.

4 JULY: Fermyn Woods is just a few miles from Oundle, and is known for being one of the top two or three sites in the country for purple emperor butterflies. Having heard that they've emerged and been seen there, I drive over on a fine, sunny morning. The wood is managed sympathetically for butterflies, and I see ringlets, a white admiral and the zesty orange wings of a silver-washed fritillary while walking along the first part of the hard forest track. The purple emperors are more elusive though. It is only after walking for about a mile that I encounter the knots of butterfly enthusiasts that tell me where they are likely to be.

The butterflies spend a lot of time high in trees, and people are searching for them through binoculars. A couple of them stop to talk to me. One had started out from Yorkshire, and visited nature reserves in Somerset and Norfolk looking for different butterflies before arriving in Northamptonshire. Another lives just a few miles away and has been walking in these woods all his life. He is very knowledgeable and happy to share his insights. I mention that the writer 'BB' (aka Denys Watkins-Pitchford) had drawn attention to the need to conserve purple emperors back in the 1960s and had reintroduced them in these woods. He tells me about other places where they have spread out naturally from a few remaining pockets of habitat. The breakthrough came when foresters stopped using certain insecticides, which allowed the caterpillar's food plant, sallows, to survive.

While we are talking, three purple emperors settle on the gravel track. If the light is at a particular angle their wings reveal a beautiful dark blue-purple colour. Otherwise they just appear dark. Their underwings are remarkably handsome, with subtle streaks of grey, brown and orange. My companion says they are males, which hatch a week before the females. They spend most of their time high up in the trees but come down to the gravel to take minerals that are important for their reproductive system. For similar reasons they also have a taste for horse and dog manure.

On the way back I smell fish at several points along the track and can't work out where it's coming from. Later I find out that rancid fish paste is used by enthusiasts to lure the butterflies down to the ground. It adds a new dimension to my view of butterflies as delicate, ethereal creatures wafting silently through the woods.

5–10 JULY: In some ways I wasn't looking forward to the annual family holiday near St David's in Wales. I knew I'd enjoy the company, and the different quality of light and sound in the landscape. But I didn't want to miss anything at home. A lot can happen in a week, especially when you've been walking the same patch of the countryside almost every day for six months. Even so, it would be good to have a change and a rest.

A highlight of the week is a walk to the eerie, isolated cove at Porthliski. Years ago I went there in the dark and spent a whole night recording waves lapping on the shore. I mixed their sounds with the drone of a windharp which I'd made to play in the soft breezes on the clifftop. This time I just sit and listen to the skittering pips and trills of the oystercatchers. On the way back I am amazed to hear the extended chuntering of a raven sitting on a rock on the clifftop. It appears to be in a conversation with a rook, and the rise and fall of its intonation sounds questioning, almost human. ◀) 7.30

Evenings on the cliffs and beaches are especially memorable. Whitesands Bay faces west and there are some glorious sunsets. My son and I go up to the cromlech on St David's Head and watch the sun go down through the prism of the standing stones. On the last evening I sit enchanted in the cathedral grounds as the rooks wheel around the ruined Bishop's Palace and settle in the stone window openings below.

On the way back to England we stop by the River Towy at Nantgaredig. The chilly water tumbles over rocks and gravel as it passes under the grey granite bridge. Occasionally a muscular salmon leaps and splashes in a slower pool at the river's edge. Then there is a familiar '*tzee!*', just loud enough to carry over the sound of rushing water, and a kingfisher tears through one of the high stone arches on its way upstream.

11 JULY: I am glad to be back in Oundle and feel excited as I walk to the bridge this morning. I see a kingfisher there for the first time in months, a startling shock of blue-green back feathers flashing in the bright sunlight above the lily pads by the water's edge. It disappears into the willows on the far bank. In April I may have

been able to pick it out again, but in July the foliage is too thick to see through.

Later in the day I return and sit for an hour on the bank, looking back towards the bridge. There is a dip in the earth where cattle go down to the water, and it makes a perfect seat among the warm leathery smell of dried cowpats. Swallows and martins sometimes swarm there in search of mud and minerals. There are none today, but a family of moorhens paddles about among the water lilies to the right.

Blackbirds sing their lazy evensong from the trees all around. I look across at the bridge's warm stone, lit by the soft first glow of sunset. There are two small arches, one pointed and the other round, designed to guide floodwaters under the bridge and take pressure off the main structure. The light picks out the irregular patchwork of sand- and grey-coloured blocks, which have been worn, restored and replaced by craftsmen across the centuries. Dates have been carved by stonemasons in different typefaces: an italic hand for repairs in 1756, roman capitals for a rebuild in 1835 and a more utilitarian style for repairs by the county council in 1946.

I imagine the scaffolding and formers that were used. There would have been sounds of sawing, scraping and chiselling, mixing of mortar, and hauling and lifting. Did the workers sing sometimes as they worked? Would I have understood their local dialects as they spoke? Hopefully the craftsmen's work was well paid and provided a decent life for their families. Perhaps the bridge had to be closed each time, and when it opened again there were celebrations involving the townsfolk and the local brewery?

Up until the 1960s there was a wharf along part of the bridge opposite where I am sitting. It was used for maintaining the reed-cutting boats that kept both the Nene and the River Welland free of vegetation. This will have been a busy place, with the sounds of metalwork and the tuning of engines.

Back in the present, the smell of charcoal barbecues floats across from the restaurant beyond the bridge. Laughter occasionally bursts from a hidden table of diners. A moorhen hoots as a heavy lorry rumbles across the roadway above. I stand up, stretch and walk away. I am unsure which century I am in. As the last blackbird sings and a kingfisher settles on a willow branch somewhere to roost through a calm and quiet night, I think about the craftsmen packing up their tools after a long, weary day and setting off for home.

12 JULY: I'm standing on the riverbank trying to identify a sound I haven't heard before, a sort of grunty '*awwwhhh*' coming from behind a willow tree. It's quite deep and sounds like a waterbird of some sort, perhaps a cormorant. Then after a few minutes a grey heron flies out. Up till now I'd only been aware of the prehistoric pterodactyl '*craaaaak*' of its flight call. It's always interesting to hear a new sound and file it away for future reference.

Later I'm sitting by the brook and hear what sounds like a mechanical drone. It's so loud I look up expecting to see one hovering right overhead. Instead, it's a huge swarm of flying ants. They appear to be the size of bees and are travelling at high speed. There are so many that it takes several seconds before they've all passed over. I'm very glad that they're flying at rooftop height, rather than closer to me on the ground. On the evening news there are reports of swarms large enough to show up on radar screens.

13 JULY: While I'm standing close to where the brook meets the river, a kingfisher flies over with a fish in its beak. It's heading in the direction of Glapthorn. I walk upstream along the brook and within a few minutes there's another fly-past. I walk more than three-quarters of a mile, stopping every now and again to watch as a kingfisher flies overhead. Eventually one veers off into a small gap where the brook's steep banks are well hidden by a thick screen of trees and bushes. A minute or two later it comes out again and heads back towards the river.

I must be fairly close to the nest by now but go no further because I don't want to disturb it. The kingfishers may have chosen this spot when the stream was still running, but by now the brook has pretty well dried up. Each day the parents are having to make up to twenty lengthy round trips to the main river to catch fish for their chicks. They also have to feed themselves and protect their territory. My admiration for them grows with each new day.

In the afternoon I go back to the millpond at Cotterstock. Loud staccato kingfisher calls come storming in from upriver, and for the next fifteen minutes there's a furious territorial display between two birds. They're making long, looping flights over a diameter of two or three hundred yards, flying up towards the lock, then heading downstream towards Tansor before whizzing back in front of the church and over the pond.

Trees block part of my view, but even when the kingfishers fly into the open they're so fast and unpredictable that I can never anticipate where a bird will appear next. First they come from this side, then that; sometimes from the front, now from the back. My mind adds in the jaguar roar of a Spitfire aircraft. There is that same juxtaposition of power and control mixed with menace as a drama plays out above the gentle green countryside of an English summer. The calls finally fade into the distance and don't return. I'm left shaking. Simply reacting to it all and trying to take in what's happening in the moment is exhausting.

14 JULY: By the river this morning I meet a young naturalist called Huw. He's just finished his school exams and is planning to do a degree in entomology. Insects aren't my strong point, so I am keen to learn as much as possible. The amount of enthusiasm, focus and detail he brings to studying a short section of the riverbank is extraordinary. He identifies a butterfly that I thought was a small skipper as an Essex skipper because the tips of its antennae are black instead of orange. And he later explains that you can tell the sexes of common blue butterflies apart because the females are brown and the males are blue.

Huw is also interested in the grasses and plants that insects live and feed on. Afterwards I look up the Essex skipper and find that it thrives on cock's-foot, tor-grass and creeping soft-grass. I had no idea there are so many varieties with such poetic names. To encounter someone who has already built up such a body of knowledge at a young age and knows exactly what they want to do with their life is inspiring, like seeing a gifted young musician with a similar drive and focus. There's a sense of endless possibilities, of a fresh mind setting out to create its own niche in the world. Huw's energy as he seeks out dragonflies and solitary wasps is a joy to watch. It is good to know that he'll be able to expand his knowledge on an academic course and hopefully have a career as a naturalist. The world needs people like Huw if it's to have a long-term future as a place worth living in.

16 JULY: Yesterday I went to the meadow by Cotterstock lock at dusk and saw a barn owl hunting. It was quartering the field, slowly flying back and forth in a regular pattern. I stood behind a small tree and eventually it came to within about thirty feet. There was no fuss and no sound. It looked like a white hologram glowing against the dark background. In some ways it reminded me of a moth flapping its wings in slow motion. It appeared just as light and insubstantial as it floated through the twilight.

This morning the hay was cut. I wonder whether the owl will be affected by this, and it seems so. It doesn't show up tonight. I can imagine that the acoustics of the cut field will have changed and made it harder to locate small mammals by their sounds. The prey may also have moved to other fields where it is easier to hide.

17 JULY: Derek is an old friend who lives on a narrowboat in the Cambridgeshire fens. He once told me that kingfishers nest every year in the bank right opposite his mooring. Today I drive over to visit him and see for myself. It is a perfect day for travelling through the flatlands, with big cloudless skies. I follow the detailed instructions he gave me involving clock towers, sharp bends and riverbanks, then pull up at the right place.

Derek's moored on the old course of the River Nene, part of a network of rivers and drainage dykes known as the Middle Level, which eventually joins the Great Ouse before flowing into the sea at King's Lynn. It is good to see him again, and we sit and talk in the hot sun on the decking beside his boat.

The river is quite narrow at this point, and the kingfisher nest is hidden in a clump of trees on the opposite side. Only one bird shows up while I am there, flying past at high speed just above the level of the far bank, but people who live in boats get to see a lot of kingfisher behaviour. Derek has some fascinating stories to tell. After his boat had been refurbished it came back with a brightly coloured painting of a kingfisher on its stern. A local kingfisher took exception to the new arrival and violently attacked the image with its beak and feet.

In spring Derek would sometimes hear banging noises and find kingfishers flying at the portholes to peck at their own reflection. He'd also seen one hovering a few yards above the water to fish. From a distance he thought it was a kestrel, then realised as he got nearer that it was a kingfisher hanging in the air like a hummingbird. Eventually it dived in and took a fish before flying off. Then there were the really magical times when Derek was sitting inside the boat with the door open and a kingfisher landed on the tiller just feet away. When it was that close he got a real sense of the wiry strength and vitality of the bird as well as its beauty.

We are sitting in a quiet spot away from busy roads. It feels very remote to me, but a couple of other narrowboats pass by as we chat. They move slowly, so the owners can acknowledge each other and exchange a few words. There is obviously a real sense of community between them, and I get the strong feeling that they might be looking at life from a different perspective. Derek asks one couple where they are heading, and they reply: "We don't know yet, but we'll be back sometime next year".

Talk shifts to music, the reason we met in the first place. I've brought along my handpan, and we play together both inside and outside Derek's boat. An accomplished singer–songwriter, he shows me an ingenious drum kit that he plays with his feet while strumming and plucking his guitar.

I come away feeling privileged to have spent time with Derek. It gives me a real insight into what it might be like to live on the old part of the river that winds through the Fens. I can imagine that life isn't always easy, and the landscape is very different from what I am used to. But we are both tuned into the moods and music of our different parts of the river, both watching and listening as the weather changes and the seasons roll past.

18 JULY: The grass has grown so tall I can only see walkers on the far bank from the waist up. The only way of telling whether they have dogs with them is by their body language. On the way back through the wood the path is dotted with feathers. All I can hear are a few quiet calls from a blackcap, chiffchaff and blackbird. When I come out into the sun again the hard green fruits of a bramble bush are starting to show. Honeybees are working among the fading blossom. There's a young fox waiting at the edge of the trees with its eyes fixed on a point on the ground. It suddenly leaps forwards and lands on all fours. I can't see whether it catches anything before it melts into the greenery and disappears.

A moment later all my tiny butterfly Christmases come at once. In a small patch of thistle and ragwort I spot a common blue, brown argus and a small copper. I've seen blues there before, but their translucent wings and evasive flit and flutter have made them hard to track against a green nettle background. Now two are settled together, and the argus and copper aren't far away. I stand and marvel at their beautifully patterned underwings.

20 JULY: As I walk through Cotterstock this morning there is a car parked by the millpond. A woman stands next to it. She is on

her own, wearing a swimmer's cap and goggles. It's not unusual to see wild swimmers there, but I am intrigued because she is playing the Last Post on a silver bugle. Whether it is a signal to other swimmers further down the river or some sort of private memorial, I'll never know. It doesn't feel appropriate to stop and ask. But she plays with great feeling, and it makes my day.

25 JULY: I haven't seen a kingfisher setting off along the brook towards Glapthorn for a couple of days. I reckon the chicks have probably left the nest there. The parents may have brought them down to the main river to learn to fish. I walk carefully through the wood along the last bit of the brook. It's dark and overgrown, and the water's only visible in places. Something makes me look back, and there's a young kingfisher perched on a thin branch no more than twenty feet away. It's sitting quietly and hasn't noticed me.

I kneel behind a tree and watch. I would never have deliberately got this close to a young bird, but as it's not alarmed it seems better to sit tight and stay still. I hardly breathe. It's clearly very young, perhaps on the first or second day out of the nest. It starts to preen itself in a methodical way, ruffling its wings so the individual feathers stand out.

Even with the naked eye it looks perfect, like a beautifully polished porcelain figurine. Birds often take time to develop their plumage but kingfishers need to be able to fly and fish straight from the nest. Their feathers have to be perfect right from the start. Preening is important. They've spent the first few weeks of their lives in an underground tunnel full of guano and fish bones, so there may be parasites which need removing too.

The kingfisher seems very interested in sounds. It cocks its head at a green woodpecker yaffle, flinches at the clash of a pigeon's wings and looks straight up towards a song thrush as it begins to sing. Its beak opens and closes a couple of times, then it heaves up a tiny white pellet that splashes in the water below.

There's a quick call as another youngster arrives and perches a few feet away. Compared to its sibling, it's noticeably thinner and more delicate. My heart goes out to it. Then there's a louder call from the river, and they both fly off with a sudden whirr of wings.

29 JULY: I kept away from the brook over the last few days in case I disturbed the fledglings. I could hear plenty of coming and going from the far side of the river. Adults flew in among the trees carrying fish. Sometimes that was every ten minutes, so it's likely that both chicks were being fed. Then over the next couple of days things got quieter, and I caught sight of one of the youngsters fishing for itself by the weir. Today I don't see them at all. They may already have moved to another part of the river.

30 JULY: Many of the natural sounds of spring and summer are fading away. The glorious chorus of blackbirds is coming to an end, and the blackcaps and chiffchaffs are singing less and less. I haven't heard a robin for quite a while. Chicks have fledged and the adults are moulting. They'll shed their worn feathers and start growing a new set for the autumn and winter. It takes up a lot of energy, and they become quiet and subdued. I'll miss their song, but it's a natural part of the cycle and they need the rest. It won't be many weeks till autumn when many birds start to sing again.

I sit for a while by the river and listen hard. There's a low drone of insects. A few birds are still singing. At the end of July 1781 Gilbert White wrote from his home in Selborne that: "The goldfinch, yellow-hammer, and sky-lark are the only birds that continue to sing". That's what I'm hearing today. There are goldfinches in the thistles, a skylark singing from the next field, and yellowhammers are calling from a hedgerow.

The distinctive sound of the yellowhammer is the one I most associate with hot summer weather. Around here, you're likely to hear them calling from roadside hedges when you drive with the car window open. Their song is traditionally remembered by the phrase: "A little bit of bread and no cheese!" but I don't hear that when I listen to the bird. The words just don't seem to fit the rhythm. I remember hearing a story about Beethoven describing in a letter how he'd listened to yellowhammers in the period before he wrote his Fifth Symphony. It could be a coincidence, but the famous opening notes of the symphony sound very like part of a yellowhammer's call to me.

I sit and listen some more, then look around. So much has changed in the past month. The leaves are a darker green now, and their undersides show silver as they rustle in the breeze. There's a smell of fermentation in the long grass after rain, and the evenings are drawing in. I can hear a horse clopping along a distant road. There's more space around the sounds, and in many ways it's easier to home in on them. That makes me more grateful than ever for what I'm hearing now, and for the soundtrack of the last few months. It's a stark reminder of what we often take for granted, and that's never a bad thing.

AUGUST

The fourth Lord Lilford   Little owl   Sparrowhawk   Badby
Poor water   Cuckoo chick   Kislingbury to Thrapston
Petrichor   Sweet unrest

1 AUGUST: I first came to the Oundle area in 1983 to set up an instrument-making workshop at Lilford Hall, an imposing Jacobean mansion set on the banks of the Nene. Before that I'd lived and worked in a small town in the dead flat Fens, so the move to rolling parklands dotted with sheep and ancient cedars was almost overwhelming. I remember coming out of my workshop one evening into a glorious pink and purple sunset. As I sat by the river, looking beyond the ruined boathouse towards the thatched buildings at Pilton, gentle ripples of church bells floated down the valley from Wadenhoe. I was completely caught up in the beauty of the moment and realised just how lucky I was.

In the nineteenth century the Hall was home to Thomas Littleton Powys, the fourth Lord Lilford. He was one of the greatest ornithologists of his time, and kept a collection of unusual and exotic birds in aviaries in the grounds, including bustards, golden eagles and bitterns. A pair of bearded vultures circled the roof and perched on the chimney stacks. He was a founding member and president of the British Ornithologists' Union and commissioned some of the best-known bird artists of the period, including Archibald Thorburn, to do book illustrations. As a member of the landed gentry he wasn't averse to shooting, but he became an early and influential supporter of the Society for the Protection of Birds in the 1890s. He also played a big part in introducing the little owl to the British Isles, which was not native here but was common in mainland Europe. He helped import some adult birds, and the first British-born little owlet was hatched on his estate in 1889.

In *A Summer on the Nene*, BB describes a visit to Lilford Hall in the 1930s when the fifth Lord Lilford was living there. There was a tropical soundscape as parrots and macaws flew free in the gardens and nested in barrels fixed in cedar trees. The bird keeper was called Mr Moody, a slow-moving man with a great affinity for birds. He kept a large collection of wildfowl on ponds near the house, including lesser white-fronted geese.

During the two years I spent at Lilford I was very busy in my workshop and hadn't yet developed a deep interest in birds. But there was still a collection of owls in the aviaries there, and I remember a magnificent eagle owl and the hatching of some snowy owl chicks. There were high-stepping cranes too, and South American rheas that made booming calls that seemed to come from the pit of their stomachs.

The park is no longer open to the public. The exotic birds have gone and the craft workshops are a distant memory. I last caught a glimpse of the Hall while paddling past in my canoe. The roof of the stable block above my old workshop had given way and was partly covered by a tattered blue tarpaulin. Chainsaws snarled at fallen trees. Past glories appear to have faded, but the descendants of the little owls introduced by the fourth Lord Lilford continue to thrive. Today they live and breed right across England and into Wales.

2 AUGUST: This evening I go to Stoke Doyle, a village a few miles away from Lilford. I've heard that a pair of little owls are nesting in a walnut tree, near some allotments that have an overgrown array of old farm equipment parked at one end. Soon after I arrive an owl flies down and perches on the steering wheel of a grey vintage tractor. It is small and delicate looking, with light speckles in its grey-brown feathers. Although no bigger than a song thrush, its appearance can be deceptive. It would still be strong enough to kill that very bird and carry it back to its nest.

At one point it lets out a quiet hiss. Then it flies up into a distant tree and stares straight at me, moving its head from side to side to get a better focus. Its face is magnetic, with pale eyebrows that make it appear bright and impish. Later another owl appears. They fly between farm roofs and fence rails until the sun goes down and their dark profiles melt into the dusk.

In her book *Owl Sense*, Miriam Darlington talks about the link between the little owl and the ancient Greek goddess Athene. The Greeks associated the owl's wakefulness and reticence with wisdom, a virtue the goddess shared. The temple at the Parthenon was dedicated to her, and was a favourite haunt of little owls. On a visit there in 1850 the young Florence Nightingale found and rescued an owlet that had fallen from its nest. She called it Athene and brought it back to England, where she nurtured and looked after it. When war broke out in Crimea she travelled there to do her nursing work. She had to leave the owl behind, but she'd already shown a far-sighted and unconventional approach to medicine by taking it with her on house calls to patients. She believed that the distraction would help their recovery.

3 AUGUST: Young birds of prey have been squeaking from the trees near Snipe Meadow for a couple of weeks, and there's one there today in the lower branches of a willow. It's quiet and passive, looking around occasionally but moving very little. When I see its staring yellow eyes I realise it's a sparrowhawk.

It shouldn't be a surprise because an adult sparrowhawk was tangling with a crow there several weeks ago, but in some ways it's unwelcome news. Sparrowhawks are fearsomely effective killers of birds up to the size of a pigeon, and are one of the few predators fast enough to catch kingfishers. I imagine their nests being lined with bright blue and orange feathers. But there's no point in being sentimental about it. Sparrowhawks need to feed their chicks too.

As if to echo my thought, a kingfisher flashes into view and settles in a tree right below where the sparrowhawk is perched. Sleek and rounded, full of life, it takes a fish with ease then passes on downriver.

5 AUGUST: I'm not complaining, but I normally only see kingfishers after standing for hours among the nettles and thistles on the riverbank or looking down from bridges. Today I spot one of the new chicks at Barnwell Park while sitting on the decking at the Kingfisher Café, coffee in hand. It is fishing from some pollarded willows in the middle of the lake and has moderate success, getting a fish on every twentieth attempt or so.

I enter a hide at the far end of the lake. There are some fellow kingfisher enthusiasts sitting inside with their cameras. One man has travelled from a big town some distance away. Following kingfishers is his main interest now that he's retired. He considers this hide the best in the county. Another photographer has been there all morning and taken some great photos. In the past they've seen kingfishers with frogs and dragonflies in their beaks.

The discussion brings home to me how valuable these sorts of observations can be. Amateurs who are out in the field regularly may notice things that scientists don't. There's a journal called *British Birds* that was founded in 1907. The archives are full of observations made by amateur ornithologists. There are reports of kingfishers eating blackberries, bacon scraps from bird tables and even of one trying to swallow a shrew. Many are from the 1920s, and I imagine them being written out in fountain pen and the letters posted in red pillar boxes all over the country.

I leave the park and walk along the road towards Barnwell lock. As I stand looking down from the bridge there's a flurry of calling. A blue streak disappears into a new nest hole about twenty yards downstream from the old one. It looks like laying may have started for a third time even before the second batch of youngsters has fully fledged and left the area. If they're successful, there should be brand-new chicks flying around well into September.

6 AUGUST: I've been getting more and more curious about the history and geography of the Nene valley upstream of Oundle. Over the next week or so I'm planning to walk from the head of the river, starting at the source and heading back towards Oundle. It's a journey of around fifty miles, so I'll take it in stages.

This morning I drive to Badby and walk downstream to Kislingbury on the outskirts of Northampton. As I set out along the Nene Way path the river is barely more than a ditch with a steady flow along its pebble bed. It is a lovely bright summer's day, and the surrounding hills are sewn in a patchwork of small fields which feel much more ancient than the flatter country around Oundle. I clamber over weathered wooden stiles and walk by hedges heavy with sloe berries. Every now and then the path winds through outlying farmyards into small village centres before returning to open countryside. Then it carries on through stubble fields slippery with chaff. The few standing barley heads are bleached ghostly white by the sun.

It's hot now, and even the rooks are subdued. From time to time I hear little scraps of wren song, the twitter of goldfinches teasing at thistle fluff and the distant thwack of cricket balls followed by polite handclaps. Sometimes the path veers away from the river and comes back after a mile or two. Each time the stream seems to have doubled in size.

After going through a gap in the hills, the river flows between the villages of Weedon Bec and Flore. By now it is big enough for paddling, and children are splashing about noisily as their parents picnic by the water. I cool my feet in it while sitting opposite an ancient stag-head oak. Its dead branches thrust up like antlers from the living green foliage.

Beyond Flore the walk begins to feel less rural. The tall white towers of Bugbrooke flour mill rise from the fields as I approach. When I get there the corrugated grain silos loom across the narrow river. There are no humans in sight, just a whine of electric motors and the chemical smell of drying paint. I crane my neck upwards, then look down again. As if to reassure me, a kingfisher takes off from a branch nearby and perches in a willow on the far side.

The path winds round the mill and through a field dotted with huge cylindrical scrap parts the size and shape of space capsules. The M1 motorway isn't far away, and the roar of traffic begins to tear at the calm I'd found in the countryside. The din gradually lessens as I walk through the meadows to Kislingbury, where children are shouting and splashing in shallow water by the old watermill. It is the sort of spot that Cromwell's army might have chosen to water their horses when they camped in the village before the battle of Naseby in 1645.

Having reached my goal for the day, I take a bus back to Badby. I feel that I've got a much better idea of how the river grows from a tiny rural spring in the hills to a larger, slower body of water moving through flatter country towards the county town of Northampton.

8 AUGUST: During my walk yesterday the river always looked clear and clean and smelled fresh. But today I look up the water-quality figures on a government website and get quite a shock. The whole stretch I walked along has a 'poor' ecological status. The fish and invertebrate numbers are healthy but chemical run-off from agriculture, roads and sewage outlets means that aquatic plants are being damaged by chemicals, even though there are no dramatic signs of pollution or discolouration.

This was unexpected. I thought the rural headwaters of the river would be in their natural state. But that's not the case in many parts of the UK. Some things may have improved since the days when rivers were heavily polluted by industry and chemicals that have since been banned. But there are growing problems caused by pressure of population and building that aren't being addressed. More investment is needed in the water and sewage system to reduce the amount of water extracted from rivers and prevent discharges of sewage into them. There are also issues with hormones, plastics and long-lasting chemicals in the water that could have long-term consequences that are currently unknown.

9 AUGUST: A few days ago I spotted a sparrowhawk chick not far from home in the trees near Snipe Meadow. Today I think I've seen another. It's perched with its back to me on a dead tree by the weir. The feathers are barred, and it's making an odd sound, a constant '*shwee-shwee-shwee*' like a distant car alarm. Every now and then a reed warbler lands on the same branch and hops right up to it before flying away. If it's a hawk that seems a strange and risky thing to do.

When I get home, I message a photo of it to Barny Dillarstone, a local friend who's very interested in birds of prey. He comes straight back to say it's a cuckoo chick. Now it becomes obvious why the reed warbler was perching so close. It's feeding a cuckoo that's several times larger than itself. This is a rare sighting, so I head straight back to the river. Barny takes some time off work and joins me soon afterwards.

The cuckoo's still near the weir and easy to spot because of its distinctive begging call. It flits between different perches, either up on the branches or in the reeds below. You can tell when it's about to be fed because the calls became louder and faster. The warbler approaches with a beak full of insects then lunges in and out of the cuckoo's gaping crimson mouth as if scared of being swallowed whole. As the young cuckoo crouches forward its thick dark body and neck became tubular so that it resembles a walrus. It's disturbing to watch, like an illustration from some dark European folk tale. The cuckoo's stance is a complete contrast to the light colour and nippy movements of its adoptive, and presumably exhausted, parent.

Eventually the odd duo fly across the river and disappear into the reeds below the weir. As we walk back towards Oundle the youngster is still calling. It seems incredible that reed warblers could be taken in by these gigantic aliens, but the cuckoo's begging call has evolved to sound like a whole nest full of hungry chicks. Most adult cuckoos fly back to Africa in June, so their offspring will never encounter them. They follow their migration instinct and discover the route to Africa entirely on their own.

10–11 AUGUST: I set out this morning to walk along the Nene for two more days, picking up where I left off, then passing through Northampton and Wellingborough on the way to Thrapston. As I drive to my starting point at Kislingbury I think about the traditional manor houses and churches that led Northamptonshire to be dubbed the county of 'spires and squires'. For an important part of the county's history there was another word beginning with 's' that made it famous: shoemakers.

The Nene valley naturally had all the raw materials needed for boot- and shoe-making. There was good grazing for the cattle that provided hides, oak forests for the bark used in tanning, and water from the river itself. Northampton developed a sizable footwear industry that was boosted in the seventeenth century when local craftsmen provided boots for Oliver Cromwell's troops. A reputation for fine work, coupled with mass production in the nineteenth century, led to the town becoming known as the shoemaking capital of the world. Red-brick factories sprang up in Northampton itself and spread down the Nene valley to Wellingborough, Kettering and Irthlingborough. By the end of Queen Victoria's reign an estimated forty per cent of the adult population in the towns worked in the trade.

As I walk into the outskirts of Northampton, I divert onto the towpath of the canal which connects the River Nene to the Grand Union. By 1761 the river was navigable from Northampton to the sea, but when the canal opened in 1815 the town was able to get cheaper coal and grain from the Midlands, and to transport goods to London more easily. This gave a further boost to the shoe industry, and the canal was still being used to carry grain to Wellingborough flour mills as late as the 1960s.

On the towpath the wind rustles in the reeds. It is hard to believe that such a quiet, narrow channel of water could have such a big effect on the town and region. In its heyday it would have been alive with working boats and the wharves further into town will have been busy. Now the canal is used by leisure boats, and is surrounded by industrial and housing estates.

At the lock where the canal joins the river, I realise that two composers for film and TV that influenced me as a child had Northampton connections. Malcolm Arnold was born there, and among many classical pieces and film scores he wrote the haunting music for the touching 1960s film *Whistle Down the Wind*. The electronic music composer Delia Derbyshire lived in the town in later life. When she worked for the BBC Radiophonic Workshop she created the *Doctor Who* theme. Its scarily insistent rhythms and unhinged theremin wails had me hiding behind the sofa for fear that daleks might burst through the screen at any moment.

After the lock, a tributary flows in from Naseby and widens the river further. Sounds echo from tall buildings and geese honk over the traffic noise. I divert along busy streets into the centre of town to visit All Saints' church. In the 1840s the poet John Clare's mental health declined and he was committed to Northampton asylum. He was allowed to walk into town from there and used to sit on a stone bench in the front porch of the church. By all accounts he was introspective and withdrawn, but he'd talk to people who recognised him. For the price of tobacco for his pipe or a glass of ale he might even write a specially commissioned poem about a special person or event in their lives.

I return to the river and walk out of town, then on through the village of Cogenhoe (pronounced 'Cuck-no'). By now the river's flowing through countryside again, though gravel is being extracted from fields close by. A stoat runs across the path as I stop by a crab-apple tree. The fallen fruit has the heady, sweet scent of cider. I pick an early blackberry from a bush and put it in my mouth. It's mouth-witheringly bitter.

The stretch of river I'm walking along now is flanked by gravel pits created by decades of open-cast extraction for road construction and housebuilding. This destroyed the original meadows and farmland but left a chain of lakes that starts at Northampton and extends downstream to Thrapston and beyond. It includes well-established reserves such as Summerleys and Titchmarsh, and is known as the Upper Nene Valley Gravel Pits. Collectively the area is a wetland of international importance for waterbirds.

At Wellingborough the Ise Brook joins the River Nene from Kettering. The water on this stretch will have been heavily polluted at the height of local shoemaking. Industry and agricultural pollution severely damaged the wildlife in the river in the 1950s and 1960s. The writer H.E. Bates was born in nearby Rushden in 1905 and spent much of his childhood with his grandparents at Higham Ferrers, within easy walking distance of the river. In *By the River* he wrote about the Nene as it would have been in the early decades of the twentieth century. He compared it to the neighbouring River Ouse, which was more natural and idyllic. The Nene was busy with barges and the colourful people who worked on them.

By now the path has become more accessible to walkers and cyclists of all kinds. I am delighted to see someone enjoying it in a motorised wheelchair, and wave back to a family with young children as they pass by on their bikes. The encounters provide respite from the inescapable drone of traffic on the nearby A45. It's a very convenient road which I often use myself, but it casts a pall of noise over a wide area.

I walk on through Stanwick Lakes, a country park that's managed by the Rockingham Forest Trust in partnership with North Northamptonshire Council. It has a strikingly modern visitors' centre and attracts people from a wide area. The different stretches of water and varied habitats are being managed for conservation, and the message is reinforced by children's activities involving wildlife.

After passing through Stanwick Lakes the path follows the line of the old railway track towards Thrapston. Although tired and footsore, I start to feel much better and can't work out why. Then I realise what has changed: the noise of the A45 is now far enough away that I can barely hear it. The air seems lighter, and my body feels less tense. As I carry on walking into a gentle breeze I can hear the music of the leaves in the different trees. A line of poplars is high-pitched, like rippling surf. A single walnut tree sounds lower and more subtle. An oak is intense, building up into waves that ebb and flow. Ash leaves shimmer like the gentle rush of water. Hawthorn is loud when I come close to it, but fades quickly as I pass.

Two horses clip-clop across a bridge further down the abandoned line. I am almost tearful with gratitude. This provides proof that the world can be quieter. The trains that used this track were noisy, but they soon passed by. The sound from a busy road is constant. People would stand at the old Ringstead station to wave as the royal train slowly went through on its way to Barnwell Castle. Today, the equivalent journey might involve the anonymous overhead roar of a helicopter.

I am surprised by the profound changes the return to natural sounds generates in me. The whole landscape looks and feels different. I eventually start to pick up noise from the approaching A14, but it seems much more manageable now that I've known some moments of peace.

13 AUGUST: As a complete change from walking I decide to spend a day in the studio sorting through some of my recent sound recordings. In contrast to the outdoor locations where they're made, I sift and sort them in a small, quiet room in front of a computer screen, wearing headphones. Sometimes the process gives me a chance to relive spring in the depths of winter. Today I'm escaping the heat of a hot summer's day and looking for somewhere cool to work.

On the computer, I press playback on some kingfisher calls, and am immediately transported back to the river where I first heard them. The calls have come out well. They're high and thin, and there's the background sound of water going over a distant weir. ◀ɔ 8.31

As an experiment, I isolate a short section a few seconds long, and slow it down and make it deeper with software so that the pitch drops by three octaves. I'm amazed at the result. It's deeper and fuller, which I'd expect, but the stretched-out sound has also become sad and poignant. It's drenched with reverberation, and there are little swoops and subtleties that the human ear could never pick up when it's going at full speed. ◀ᴖ 8.32

It has a lot in common with the eerie howls of wolves and the sounds whales make underwater. I email a short sample to a friend. She tells me that when she played it her dog began barking and ran out of the room.

16 AUGUST: This morning I drive to Thrapston to walk the final section downriver to Oundle. It's around here that the pronunciation of the River Nene changes, even though the spelling stays the same. Upriver it's pronounced 'Nen'. Downstream it's 'Neen'. I've not come across a good explanation why, but it's very important to the people on either side of the division. Perhaps it marks a tribal border from a long time ago.

On the riverside, there is an information board about a local man, Sir John Washington. He was the great-great-grandfather of George Washington, the first President of the United States. Many pilgrims set out from the Nene valley to America. They included the ancestors of the Presidents John Adams and John Quincy Adams, and of the inventor and statesman Benjamin Franklin.

The path passes by the beautiful old watermill and then reaches a series of flooded gravel pits that have been turned into Titchmarsh nature reserve. At one of the bird hides I stop to watch some cormorants and the slow flight of a great egret. On the far side of the lake is an old duck decoy that was originally constructed by the fourth Lord Lilford in 1885. It's now a heronry, home to a large number of breeding grey herons in the nesting season in February each year.

I walk on to Wadenhoe. The church there is elevated on a small escarpment in an idyllic setting, but I am sad to see a number of prohibitive signs by the river. The growth of wild swimming, paddleboarding and canoeing has resulted in a lot of the traditional access points along the river being shut off. The river is free for all to use, but there are few places left locally where you can dive into it or launch a craft.

As the path crosses the fields towards Stoke Doyle, the elegant profile of Lilford Hall is across the river to the right. A mile or so later I am back on home territory, sitting on the jetty at Barnwell lock, cooling my feet in the water. As a narrowboat goes by I notice a small brass sculpture of a kingfisher perched on the swan-necked tiller arm that reaches out behind the steerer. It peers down into the boat's wake.

I walk on down the river to Ashton. A brief flash of blue back feathers disappears into the trees opposite the lock. I stop and wait. A brown hawker dragonfly flies through some burdock heads with a dry crackle of dusty wings. Wood pigeons coo. There's a creaky yaffle from a green woodpecker upstream.

A light wind blows a scatter of white clouds across the sky. Sunlight bounces off the river, sending ripples of light along the lichened branches of an ash tree on the far bank. Back at the bridge in Oundle a tiny patch of blue is showing through the leaves of a tree by the boathouse. The kingfisher takes off as I pass, flying off across the meadows towards the trees downriver.

20 AUGUST: It's raining hard this morning. There's a sweet scent in the air that rises from the earth when rain comes after a dry spell. It even has its own name: *petrichor*. It's partly caused by plant

oils that become absorbed in the soil and released when the rain disturbs it.

I sit under an overhanging ash tree. Raindrops send circular ripples across the water. Larger drips from the tree's leaves spawn half-bubbles which briefly pop up like space-helmeted frogs then, just as suddenly, disappear. I watch them for a while then set off home through the gentle patter of trees dripping onto the forest floor.

The sun comes out in the afternoon, and I head back to the meadows. Now the scent is even more heady. I stop to sniff at some of the leaves and flowers along the way. Bindweed has no smell at all. Nor does purple loosestrife, which is surprising given the beauty of its flowers. Mint is predictably calming, and when I rub the leaves on my forehead it feels cool.

I stop at a tall patch of Himalayan balsam. The flowers are pink and swarming with bees, but as an alien species the plant isn't always popular with naturalists. I can't smell the flower, but when I crush some petals between finger and thumb there's a hint of peach. Nettles smell dark green and bitter. A blue thistle head comes close to having a scent like a garden flower. Most aromatic are the yellow flowers of common ragwort.

When I reach the woods, I head for a gap in the trees to get a view up and down the river. A full canopy of summer leaves can make a wood a dark and gloomy place, and I'm attracted to the light of the sky and its reflection in the water. Cuckoo-pint, also known as lords-and-ladies, is dotted along the path. Its red berries are like little waymarkers. Back in the meadows the gate slams behind me with a loud, punctuating click. I notice an orange and light brown shape settled on a fence rail. Appropriately, it's a gatekeeper butterfly.

25 AUGUST: At lunchtime I take a sandwich to Lower Barnwell lock, hoping to sit and relax as the river flows by. But as I arrive two kingfishers put on a virtuoso display of flying. They come within a few yards of each other by the lock, then separate and make wide, wheeling turns through the trees and back again in overlapping circles. It's a blur of unexpected changes of direction with orange underbodies alternating with the blue of their upperwings.

Then one lands high in a tree and waits with head cocked. It gives me a chance to take my camera out until the other arrives, calling loudly, and there are more explosive looping flights followed by perching further down the bank. This happens repeatedly for nearly an hour before they both fly off upstream.

It looks like a courtship display, but when I get home the photos show that both the birds were males. They could have been young birds having a dispute over territory. The whole thing was so captivating that I realise I forgot to eat the sandwich.

28 AUGUST: Robins have started to sing again, and they won't stop till next summer. Even on the harshest winter day you're likely to hear that silvery voice. And other birds have begun to break their late-summer silence, including chiffchaffs and dunnocks.

A pair of buzzards wheel and call high overhead as I get to the wood. It reminds me of a recording I made here a couple of months ago. ◀ 8.33

I cut down towards the river, along a path that's overgrown with nettles and brambles. As it gets closer to the water it's wetter underfoot but easier to get through. Just as I get to the river a kingfisher leaves an invisible perch in the overhanging willows. One of its calls is only ten feet away as it passes, and I hear a couple in a canoe downstream call out in surprise as it flies right by them.

31 AUGUST: There's a real sense that summer is ending. I get out my copy of *The Wind in the Willows*, a book I come back to again and again. In among the well-known characters and their enjoyable adventures are some breathtaking insights into nature, and there's a magical sense of place and time. In the chapter 'Wayfarers All', it's late summer and Ratty is restless: "There's an air of change and departure. Birds are feeling the call of the South". He meets three swallows who are making plans for their journey. Ratty asks why they have to go – isn't their home here good enough for them?

They talk of "a sweet unrest" and describe how "one by one the scents and sounds and names of long-forgotten places come gradually back and beckon to us". Ratty asks why, if those places are so good, will they bother coming back next year? They answer that in due course the season will call them back to lush meadows, the cuckoo's call, and "quiet waterlilies swaying on the surface of an English stream. But to-day all that seems pale and thin and very far away. Just now our blood dances to other music."

Such an eloquent evocation of the dreams of autumn and the dreams of spring. And such wonderful words to read at the cusp of the seasons, when summer starts to tip over into autumn with all the changes, mysteries and uncertainties that will bring.

SEPTEMBER

BB at Cotterstock   Owls in B flat   Swallows   Loud voices
Rain in the wood   Dawn at Barnwell   Yew   Harvest moon
Subsong   Bell-ringing   The sign   A starburst of kingfishers

1 SEPTEMBER: I've been rereading a chapter in *A Summer on the Nene* where BB describes tying his boat up at Cotterstock and visiting the church. He was very taken by an incised carving of two deer inside the fifteenth-century porch. When I get to the village this morning, I decide to take a look. I walk up past the mill, which was still working when the book was written, and along an avenue of lime trees. I open the wrought-iron gate to the churchyard and scrunch down the gravel path. A flock of pied wagtails parts in front of me and hops about among the graves and crosses.

There are many initials and dates on the stone walls of the porch, some dating back to the eighteenth century. It takes a while to find the deer. They are high up by a window opening, scratched in the soft yellow stone with an old nail or key. I step onto a low stone seat and trace them with my fingers. They feel rough and uneven, and have the timeless look of ancient cave drawings.

The porch is little more than ten feet square, with a low vaulted ceiling decorated by stone corbels of regal figures and mythical beasts. A dried-mud nest clings to the stonework. The rounded heads of two young swallows poke out like comical medieval friars peering from a pulpit. Their parents carry on feeding them while

I'm there, flying into the porch with a screech and stuffing insects into the yellow gape of their beaks.

The porch offers some shelter, but it has no door and the window openings are unglazed, so it's open to wind and weather. Shadows sharpen as the sun comes out. A cool breeze blows through from the river to the east. On other days there will be west winds from the direction of the forest. The young swallows' first flight will be a short hop into the churchyard. Then before long they'll be taking off beyond the gravestones on a perilous journey south to Africa lasting many weeks and covering six thousand miles.

3 SEPTEMBER: I'm walking from Oundle towards Cotterstock, light failing, footsteps falling on the hard clay path. There's a faint breeze in my face and the electric fizz of grasshoppers in the long, dry grass. Tawny owls hoot from the hedgerows. A muntjac barks. A dog joins in from a farm near Glapthorn.

Senses sharp in the darkness, I slip through the wood to the river and lean against a tree. The ivy rustles. The riverbank smells of hay and horses. There's the shriek of a grey heron downstream. A star sways and dances in the water. Bats criss-cross, taking insects.

I tiptoe back among tree roots to the path, ducking branches. More tawny calls, more grasshoppers. I'm almost at the rugby pitch on the edge of town. There's a commotion in the nettles to my left, and the black and white face of a badger peers out. He stomps off down the path then crashes back into the brambles.

Four teenage boys sit on a bench by the rugby club. They're hunched over their phone screens with their backs to me, unaware that I'm slipping by in the dark. Two men play tennis in a dazzle of floodlights. As I get into bed an owl calls from the garden. He's still there when I wake in the night.

5 SEPTEMBER: Today is one of those warm, still and sunny days you always hope for in September. Robins, chiffchaffs and tits are calling along the river. There are butterflies in the woods and long grasses, berries in the hedgerows, and wild hops weave through the hawthorn by the millpond.

At dusk, I go up to the edge of Southwick Forest. A trio of ravens circles above the Bulwick road. When I get to the forest track a nightingale starts *wheet*-ing and growling for a couple of minutes just as dusk falls. I'd have thought it should have set for the south by now, but the sound is clear and unmistakable. I hear no response from another nightingale, but soon afterwards a tawny owl starts to call right above my head. Another answers from not far behind me.

What follows is an exchange of some of the most beautiful and evocative owl calls I've ever heard. They are loud and close enough to hear the subtleties of sound and tone that get smoothed out by reflections off trees in the night air. What strikes me most is how like medieval recorders and organ pipes they sound, almost to the point that I wonder if the instrument makers and players of the time might have listened to them for inspiration. ◀) 9.34

Gilbert White compared the tawny owl's hooting note to a "fine vox humana", an effect created on organs where two pipes of the same note are deliberately tuned slightly differently to one another. The result is a subtly trembling sound that's thought to resemble the human voice. White also tried to work out the pitch of their calls using a set of wooden organ pipes that provided the notes to tune harpsichords. He decided that: "Most owls seem to hoot exactly in B flat". I can imagine him in the parlour of his home at night, opening the window and softly blowing pipes of different lengths until he got an answering call from the walnut trees.

He wasn't far out with the note. Standards of pitch changed in the nineteenth century, when instrumentalists began to play higher so they could be heard more easily, but the longer owl hoots that I am listening to are tuned in B flat too.

7 SEPTEMBER: The swallows have gone. There were scores of them skimming the river for insects yesterday but not today. I stand by the millpond looking towards the church but there are none there either. The young chicks only left their nest in the church porch a couple of days ago. If they've set off south too, then good luck and Godspeed. At least they've started in light winds and good weather.

It makes me feel sad, but there are plenty of things to compensate. So many white butterflies flutter around me on one stretch of the river path that I could be a princess in a Disney cartoon. There are more speckled wood butterflies on the feather-lined path through the spinney than I've ever seen before.

The chiffchaffs seem to raise their volume by the day, and there's a blackcap singing from a tree just overhead. I stand and listen to it quietly singing to itself. All the beauty with none of the bravado.

10 SEPTEMBER: For the second day running it rained in the night, and this morning's southern breeze is warm and soupy. Yesterday it reminded me of fresh bread and honey. Today there's camomile and spice mixed in too.

When I get to Cotterstock lock a cormorant is standing with its wings spread out to dry in the sun. I'm just thinking that I haven't heard or seen a kingfisher for a couple of days when one starts calling from the trees about seventy yards downriver. Another answers from the bank just behind me. They never break cover, but there's a minute or two of high-pitched, high-speed calling that sounds like Morse code bouncing back and forth between them.

When I get to the pond a pair of kestrels mews and circles overhead, scattering the pigeons on the church roof. Near the edge of town there's a headscarfed lady picking blackberries. There are plenty of berries there, and I keep meaning to gather some myself. But I mustn't leave it too long. As my mother tells me every year, drawing deep on her Dorset roots: "You can't pick blackberries past the end of September 'cos the Devil's piddled on 'um!"

13 SEPTEMBER: I stand on the riverbank looking across at the trees, thinking how beautifully the birds are singing again. After the silence of the moult a different voice seems to join in every day. The volume's nowhere near as loud as the spring chorus but there are wrens and robins, chiffchaffs, tits of all kinds and a quiet but insistent blackcap. Wood pigeons, crows and red kites are in the background too.

Then I hear human voices, and two single canoes appear round a bend in the river. The paddlers are shouting to each other even though they're only a few yards apart. There's the deep, bawling tone of alpha males sharing in physical exertion. They paddle quickly by in a clamour of office politics. As their noise recedes, I go back to giving the birds my full attention. But there's nothing to hear. They've stopped singing.

I'm genuinely alarmed, thinking something might have happened to my hearing. I walk along the bank, clicking my fingers next to each ear to check. Then I walk back to where I started. Very gradually the birds start to sing again. I take a long, deep breath of relief. Not long afterwards, there's the gentle swish and putter of a narrowboat. Three elderly gentlemen are gathered at the front while another steers at the rear. They look like cast members from the long-running British sitcom *Last of the Summer Wine*, which follows the gentle escapades and adventures of a retired group of friends with time on their hands. They're silently munching on thick white-bread sandwiches and trailing the smell of frying bacon in their wake.

This time the birds just keep on singing.

14 SEPTEMBER: It's a proper rainy day, so I put on waterproofs from the neck down but top it off with a flat cap. It'll soon get sodden, but half the fun of being out in the rain is listening to the raindrops. Any sort of hood distorts and diminishes the sound.

The patter of rain on the river sounds like the calls of a distant flock of shorebirds or starlings. The birds themselves are mostly silent, just a few coarse rooks and the dry chatter of a magpie from the wood. In Cotterstock I stop and listen where a stretch of trees and foliage have recently been trimmed and cleared. The gentle sound of rain on leaves has been replaced by splashes on the black plastic put down to deter weeds. It's a whole different soundscape from a year ago.

There are flurries of sound as I pass under the sycamores stretched out along the path to the wood. When I get to the entrance, I plunge in. Goodness, it's dark! It's only mid-morning but could easily be dusk. There are drips and drops at every level, from treetops to boughs, branches to leaves and twigs, and then onto the forest floor. I'm surrounded by them, surfing on them. There's more leaf-fall on the path now, and it's slick and slippery underfoot. When I get to a dry patch, I stop to find out why. It's sheltered by a tangle of overhanging ivy, something to look out for when I'm caught in the rain with no proper clothing.

It's a day for mushrooms and fungi. There's a tall willow whose trunk is bedecked with fungus. It's a magnificent sight. I count the rungs of a surreal pixie ladder of shell shapes that grow up and out of the bark. There are at least fifty, and they have the texture and colour of bread or pizza dough.

As I leave the wood the tree sounds fade and I stop to look at blackberries in a hedgerow. The drops bounce through them but hang in long lozenges from the rose hips close by. I look up the tree fungus when I get home, and it's called chicken of the woods.

16 SEPTEMBER: I wake early on a still morning and go to Barnwell Country Park before six to make some sound recordings. It's still dark when I arrive, but rooks are already cackling in the trees and there are a few hesitant calls from a tawny owl. As a church clock strikes six there's a '*peewit*' from a lapwing and a cock crows towards Stoke Doyle. Robins start their ticking sounds then settle into song. A family of geese swims by. The young call amid the abrasive honks of the adults, which speeds up when a group takes off with the thresh of webbed feet against water. Their cries fade into the distance. A grey heron flies by with a screech. ◀ 9.35

As the low sun starts to pick out the trees on the far side of the lake, the first kingfisher comes sweeping in from the right and wheels into an opening in the willows near the water's edge. The chicks have come out of the nest and moved to the lake. I can hear their sibilant calls, like two coins being clinked together. After a barrage of high, reedy clicks and calls a line of five kingfishers flies past from right to left just in front of me. 🔊 9.36

I walk round the lake, looking down among the overhanging willows, and catch a glimpse of a chick perched close by. The light's still low and behind it, so there are no colours showing. As it turns its head and long beak to look back over its shoulder the profile is like one of those toy woodpeckers that nods as it slides down a wire pole.

The day warms and brightens, and there are little flurries of calls as two chicks settle on some bare branches about seventy yards away from where I'm sitting. Occasionally they attempt to fish, but they are still being visited by an adult, which lands on a branch nearby and feeds them at lightning speed before winging off across the water.

18 SEPTEMBER: This morning there's a small cross section of a yew branch on the pavement in Cotterstock. I stoop to pick it up and it fits neatly in my palm. It weighs about the same as an apple and smells of coal tar soap. I count the growth rings on its rough sawn surface. It sprouted from the trunk before I was born.

Historically prized for its strength and resilience, yew wood was used to make longbows. It was also turned into musical instruments, and I've used it myself to build the curved staves that make up the delicate pear-shaped back of a lute. When the timber's first planed and scraped it reveals a wonderful range of colours, from the cream of the sapwood through to light pinks, oranges and purples. It sands and polishes beautifully till it's perfectly smooth to the touch.

A group of crows circles overhead, and I hear the gruff call of a raven towards Perio Barn Farm. Raven quills were used to make plectra, the parts of a harpsichord that pluck the strings when a note on the keyboard is pressed down. It's easy to forget that people were making things for millennia before synthetic materials arrived, and how much was achieved with natural products combined with the wisdom and skill to get the best from them.

21 SEPTEMBER: The dawn before equinox starts off cool and misty. Crooks of bare branches are spun with dew-pearled spiders' webs. It soon changes as a gentle west wind brings warm scents and golden sunlight. Chiffchaffs call down from the trees, and a pair of grey wagtails flits on the lichened bridge by the pond. Craneflies rise from the grass, and every glance towards the low sun is filled with the bob and sway of their wings. Ivy flowers hum with bees, and a red admiral rests in a small patch of sunlight.

I sit by the river and wait. Eventually a silent kingfisher flies in from upstream. For a moment it looks to be landing in the reeds opposite, but it veers away and settles further downstream. It calls a couple of times. I wait a while longer, just enjoying the moment, then set off for home.

I come back to the same spot at dusk to wait for a full harvest moon. I've watched a lot of sunrises, but this will be my first moonrise. It's darkening fast as the sun dims in the west. A smudge of light appears to the northeast. Tawny owls call as an orange disc rises slowly from the horizon. Layers of dust and cloud scatter the light to warm the colours of the low night sky. The moon passes imperceptibly slowly through the leaves of a small tree on the far bank, and when it finally breaks free there's a real change in the quality of the light. I hold one hand in front of the other, and moonlight throws shadow fingers against my palm. I kneel on the cool bare earth to watch the moon reflect in the water. It's brighter and more yellow now, swaying in the circular dimples made by rising fish. A moth whirrs past my right ear, and a grey heron calls to the left.

There are voices from behind. Two lights, head-torch high, make their way along the path. I wait to see if they'll come close, then call out: "Good evening!" There are two pleasant replies, the voices of young lads. They carry on past without stopping. Good luck to them. There are plenty of dips and roots on the path. It's not easy to walk so close to the river even in daytime.

My eyes slowly readjust to the moonlight. I start to walk back through the trees to the main path on the other side of the wood. There are spots of light in places, but I mostly go by sound and feel. If I stray from the bare earth of the twisting path the scuff of leaves and scrub underfoot tells me something is wrong. Each front foot slides close to the ground feeling for roots or rabbit holes.

I come out of the trees to the edge of the stubble field. It's pitch dark to start with, then moonlight starts to filter through gaps in the foliage and reach across the path itself. I stop in a pool of light and my shadow stretches out long and thin. I pace out fifteen steps from where I was standing to where the top of my head had been on the ground. That makes my shadow eight times taller than me.

As I get to the end of the trees I look down towards the meadows and there's a low mist on the river. The moon has a blue tinge with a faint aura of rainbows. Its light softens the landscape into mauve and yellow forms mixed with brown. The rugby pitch was lit and busy when I passed by earlier. Now it's deserted, and the short grass shines in the moonlight.

I get up in the night and the garden's an eerie white. The moon is high, clear and silver. Its seas are a deep dark grey. Tree shadows are short and scissor sharp. A calm, clear start to the autumn equinox.

22 SEPTEMBER: I'm sitting on the swing seat in the garden on another gloriously warm and sunny day. Suddenly my ears home in on a tiny sound, like a distant blackbird singing its heart out on a May evening. Except it's coming from a box hedge fifteen feet in front of me. It's the quiet subsong of a blackbird singing to itself. I sometimes hear it on a sunny day in the depths of winter, usually from deep in an evergreen tree or shrub. But I've never heard it this early in the autumn.

It's a complete delight. All the familiar warbling tones tumble out in a long liquid stream. I don't know how they get such a beautiful tone. All the birds I've been lucky enough to see doing this were singing with their beaks closed throughout. It's a virtuoso display with a tiny voice. Research shows that birds learn songs by improvising, burbling in a non-specific way, then picking out phrases that they like and repeating and building on them. That sounds a lot like what is going on here. It's also how I compose on an instrument, noodling about and letting my hands daydream until something comes out that's worth developing into a piece of music.

It never ceases to amaze me how many natural sounds I'm still hearing for the first time. I've missed so much in the past. This is one I'll be listening out for again. And I won't wait till the depths of winter next time.

23 SEPTEMBER: I go back to Barnwell to see how the chicks are faring. I can hear four or five calling from different parts of the lake and see them flying together in single file. They're attempting to fish for themselves and during a couple of hours I never see an adult feeding them. I'm puzzled that they're still here. It's generally thought that the parents chase the young birds off their territory after four days. Maybe there's enough fish to go round.

25 SEPTEMBER: There is an extended bout of bell-ringing from St Peter's church this afternoon so I walk there to investigate. I'm glad I do, as a group of bell-ringers have travelled from as far as London and Bristol to spend their weekend ringing in as many local churches as possible.

This is by no means their first church of the day. They've just finished a quarter peal when I arrive, which means they had performed 1,250 changes with the eight bells. A full peal would have taken three hours. They do a final five minutes to "put the bells to bed" and make sure to leave the bells in the up position.

Then they stagger down the narrow, uneven stairs from the church tower. Many are elderly, with sweat patches on their shirts and hair sticking up around their heads. True enthusiasts.

Change ringing is an English tradition. It's the art of ringing a set of tower bells in a series of mathematical variations. The bells were silenced during wartime when they were reserved for raising the alarm if there was an invasion. They were also silent during the lockdown caused by the Covid-19 virus. But otherwise it's hard to imagine the countryside without them.

There are a handful of human sounds that can enhance a birdsong recording. The sound of children playing in the distance is one. Another is the whistle of a distant steam train. A brass band playing at a village fete might be another. But for me the sound of distant church bells is the most evocative of all. One of my dreams is to capture a nightingale singing with bells in the background. I've not managed this so far, but I once recorded a robin singing outside a local village church during bell practice. 🔊 9.37

27 SEPTEMBER: I was born near the sea and always perk up when the weather's a bit wild. I dress up this morning in waterproofs and a flat cap then plunge into the wind and rain. It stops five minutes later and the sun comes out. It stays out. There's a glorious, rain-washed sky and a range of life, light and colour on the trees and meadows that's been missing for a long time.

In the woods there's wind and movement at every level, from treetops to forest floor. It's totally different from the stasis of the last couple of weeks. I brave the nettles and brambles of the overgrown path along the river. The waterproofs come in useful as protection against scratches and stings. There are lots of slippery roots underfoot, and walking requires balance and concentration. At the last minute a large and unyielding bramble reaches out from behind me and grabs the cap off my head.

In Snipe Meadow the sun sparkles off the bend in the river. At the tennis courts a coach shouts to his student: "Open your shoulders out as wide as you can!" It sounds like good advice, in life as in tennis.

28 SEPTEMBER: There's an oblong metal sign by the riverside footpath that states: "No trespassing, by order". Below it there's a long list of other dos and don'ts. At the moment it's unreadable

because the words are overgrown by delicate swags of honeysuckle. It's as if the subversive scribe of an illuminated medieval manuscript has deliberately set out to obscure what he's written. A pair of red admiral butterflies is settled on one of the few visible words. They're bright emojis of joy and hope protesting against the dull dead hand of human bureaucracy.

30 SEPTEMBER: I'm sitting at the edge of the lake at Barnwell. I can hear two kingfisher chicks hidden away on either side of me and can just make out two tiny orange shapes on a dead branch at the far side of the lake. They're still trying to master the art of fishing, and every now and then one plops into the water and returns with nothing. Many young kingfishers become waterlogged during their attempts to fish, and drown. Life is hard, and the water isn't the only danger. I saw a sparrowhawk dip towards one yesterday as it flew back up to its perch. The youngster instinctively veered off, flying low across the surface so the hawk couldn't catch it. It's estimated that only half the chicks survive beyond two weeks, and just a quarter will still be alive to breed next year.

The parents still seem to be feeding them, but less and less each day. One flies in from the right and settles on the dead branch. A noisy melee of fluttering chicks flies in from different parts of the lake and forms into a line next to it. I lift up my camera and start taking pictures. When the nearest has been fed they all fly off in different directions.

I look at the digital screen. One of the images has captured the blue and orange starburst of their parting. I feel in my pocket and there's a jingle of pound coins. Enough for a coffee. I head off for a celebratory drink at the Kingfisher Café.

OCTOBER

By the millpond   A trip to Fotheringhay   Woodpecker
Ludwig Koch   The conker championships   A walk to Helpston
Badger   Rutting stag   Raindrops   Autumn leaves   Clocks
change   An almighty storm

1 OCTOBER: I'm sitting by the millpond, trying to deal with the chilly thought that the swallows won't be back till spring. I take a deep breath, look around and listen. The sun comes out. Yellow leaves flicker in the hedgerows. A wren whirrs in the reeds. Grey wagtails skip along the stone parapet and a red kite circles the church tower. Then I imagine that the departing swallows left brightly coloured trails in the sky that curve and crackle like distant fireworks. A kingfisher flies under the bridge and sits on a willow branch. Its feathers shimmer in the sunlight, and my heart lifts and sings.

3 OCTOBER: I'm paddling my canoe from Oundle to Fotheringhay. It's a calm day, and the air smells of rush mats and woodsmoke. Willow leaves and pale blue skies reflect off the river's mirrored surface. A kingfisher sits on a post by Tansor church. It doesn't move as I drift past. When I look back, it's still there, head tilted towards the water, waiting for a fish.

I get out at Perio lock. A pair of kingfishers chases over the weir and veers off through the trees. I hear them calling as I lift the canoe back in and float past the houseboats by Bluebell Lakes.

The octagonal lantern tower of Fotheringhay church rises from the fields to the left. It's sharp edged in the clear light, topped by the gleaming shape of a falcon and fetterlock. It's seems very grand for a parish church, but Fotheringhay is no ordinary village. It has royal links going back to the thirteenth century and Richard III was born there in 1452.

I pass under the stone bridge and clamber onto the bank near the grassy mound of Fotheringhay Castle. Mary Queen of Scots, a Catholic, spent the last part of her nineteen-year imprisonment here. She was beheaded in the castle's hall in 1557 on the orders of her Protestant cousin Elizabeth. At the time she was at the centre of European religious rivalry and politics. News of her death sent shock waves across the Channel and helped trigger the Spanish Armada less than a year later.

All that remains of the building today is a fenced-off pile of masonry down by the river. I climb the steep mound and sit on a tussock of grass, trying to picture the site in Elizabethan times. It's set above flat meadows on the edge of Rockingham Forest. It was chosen as Mary's prison because floods and marshy land would make it difficult for her supporters to free her.

I look down at the river heading east towards the Fens and think about the scents and sounds of the time: the smell of dung and hay, rotting vegetables, cooking smoke, the reek of foul water in the moat. There will have been sounds of woodland birdsong; the cries of geese and curlews flying along the river; owl hoots and rutting stags; horses, farm animals and cocks crowing; people talking, calling, shouting and singing.

Mary was heavily guarded during her imprisonment, but she was allowed many of the trappings of a royal court. Rich food was served. There may have been music too, hunting horns and fanfares but also more refined ensembles and songs. She was an accomplished musician, playing the lute and virginals. There's a small wire-strung harp with beautiful Celtic carvings in the National Museum of Scotland, in Edinburgh, known as the 'Queen Mary Harp', which she's said to have given to a famous harpist. It's also known that the composer and instrumentalist James Lauder followed Mary from the Scottish court and played during her imprisonment. Recorders, lutes and viols may have provided a gentle and welcome distraction. She and her household also created exquisite pieces of embroidery and needlework.

Mary was eventually implicated in a plot to kill Elizabeth and take the throne for herself. She was tried in the castle in October 1586 and executed there the following February. Her tragic life and death in Fotheringhay inspired many works of art and music across Europe and beyond. The German poet Schiller wrote a play about her which was adapted into the opera *Maria Stuarda* by the Italian composer Donizetti. Robert Burns wrote a lament, while the English folk singer Sandy Denny composed and recorded a song about her in the 1960s.

I leave the castle site and walk down the village's only street. The road's unusually wide, reflecting its greater importance in the past. I turn up the drive to the church and step inside. It's a large building with a fine acoustic. Its royal and monastic connections mean that religious music performed here will have been of a high standard. The second Duke of York was buried in the church after being killed at the battle of Agincourt in 1415. In 1476 King Edward IV came to Fotheringhay for the entombment of his father Richard, Duke of York, and his brother Edmund. It was one of the most spectacular events of his reign, and five thousand people came to the church to receive alms. Many more attended a dinner held at the castle and in the tents and pavilions pitched around it.

It's hard to imagine that today. I'm the only person in the building. Light's flooding through the clear glass windows. It's quiet, but every little movement I make is picked up and amplified by the walls. I sing a few notes and my voice takes on an ethereal bloom that makes it sound like a whole choir of monks. Something about the space and its acoustic makes me feel very emotional.

In 2014 the singer-songwriter Kerry Devine used this church to record a CD of songs inspired by her native Fens. She first visited the building to perform at a wedding and felt that the sound captured a sense of longing she associates with the fenland landscape. She returned to sing and record with her musicians over several evenings, setting up microphones around the church to capture as much of that sound and feeling as possible. I can hear her beautiful soaring voice as I look up towards the oak beams of the main church and the intricate fan-vaulted ceiling of the tower.

When I get back to the riverbank there's a lady paddling by in her canoe. We've passed each other before on the river and swapped sightings of birds. She calls out that she thinks she just saw five kingfishers flying in a row further down the river towards Warmington. She can't really believe it. Can that be possible? I'm delighted to tell her that it is. It'll be a late brood of chicks. The river's alive with them just now. It's so wonderful that other people are seeing them too.

4 OCTOBER: There's a great spotted woodpecker in a tree about seventy yards away. I can just make out its angled profile among

the branches. I walk carefully towards it and stop. Then I walk slowly forward, a few paces at a time, feet tracing the ground with a minimum of fuss and movement. I finish up about ten yards away, surprised that it's not reacted and flown away. I take in its sharp-beaked profile and bright, contrasting feathers that remind me of an old-fashioned sailor decked out in a red cap and black and white tailcoat.

It's unusual to see a woodpecker like this, so close and so still. They're usually a blur of movement as they wind around a trunk or branch, tapping in search of food. I don't want to alarm it, so carefully back off and return the way I've come. When I get to the bridge and look back it's still there, poised at a jaunty angle against the bare trunk of the last tree in the hedgerow.

6 OCTOBER: I often carry a small handheld sound recorder in my pocket. It came in handy this morning when I saw a green woodpecker fly up from the ground into a large willow tree. The bird has a distinctive laughing call that it doesn't repeat often. It's hard to anticipate, and I don't have many examples. I put the recorder on top of a tree stump, switch it on and wait. Luckily there is another call within a couple of minutes. I check on headphones that I managed to capture it then carry on walking. ◄) 10.38

Recording birdsong is simpler than it used to be. Good equipment is relatively cheap, light to carry and easy to use. The pioneer of wildlife recording was Ludwig Koch. As a young boy in 1889 he made the world's first known recording of a bird when his wealthy father gave him an Edison wax cylinder machine as a present. He fled from Nazi Germany in the 1930s and settled in England, where the biologist Julian Huxley gave him help and encouragement. Koch set out to make the first commercially available collection of birdsong recordings: *Songs of Wild Birds*.

Mobile recording at that time needed heavy equipment that had to be carried in a large van. It was done on shellac discs that could only record for a short period and were very fragile. Assistants had to reel out hundreds of yards of electrical cables when the van couldn't get close enough to the birds. The commercial discs were released in 1936 as a 'sound book' with text and photographs. One of the tracks is a single call from a green woodpecker which took two whole weeks to record. That's quite a contrast to the ease with which I got my recording. The quality of Koch's disc is excellent for the time, but there are continuous background crackles that sound distracting to modern ears.

Koch wanted his recordings to be useful to ornithologists and birdwatchers but also to anyone who could appreciate the beauty and relaxing effect of the sounds themselves. He described birds as "the most... uplifting and artful of all living things". His BBC broadcasts about bird sounds became very popular with both children and adults. They fitted in with the principles of the corporation's founder Lord Reith, who saw its mission as to "inform, educate and entertain". During wartime they also played a part in raising morale by creating a sense of a heritage and countryside worth fighting for.

Koch wrote an autobiography, *Memoirs of a Birdman*, and his work inspired many amateurs to record birdsong. A Bristol woman called Pamela Fursman made a collection of tapes between the 1940s and 1960s which is archived in the town's museum. I remember listening to programmes on BBC radio in the 1970s which featured wildlife recordings sent in by amateur recordists. I was fascinated by the idea of doing some myself. It was a while before I got around to it, but I'm glad I did. And I very much appreciate being able to whip a handheld recorder out of my pocket the moment I hear something interesting.

8 OCTOBER: Recently, I remembered that Colin, a friend who lives locally, had mentioned buying some 78 rpm discs that included recordings made by Ludwig Koch. I knew he also had a collection of old gramophones, so got in touch to see if I could listen to them being played on the sort of machine that was popular when they were first released. I visit his house today, and we both go up to the study where he keeps his recordings and equipment. The discs themselves are from the original *Songs of Wild Birds* series Koch brought out in 1936. They feel heavy, even though each side contains only a few minutes of sound. The carboard sleeves they come in are simple and unadorned.

Colin plays them on an HMV 109 wind-up gramophone with a beautifully polished mahogany case. It has no electrical parts, and the vibration from the needle is amplified by a built-in horn. We start by listening to a nightingale, and I am impressed by the realistic tone and variation in the sound. It also strikes me that the ritual of winding up the gramophone, taking the disc out of its sleeve, carefully placing it on the turntable, and delicately dropping the tone arm and needle in the right place made listening much more of an event and performance. At the time the discs came out it was the only way to experience wild birdsong all year round inside the home. That will have made it very special indeed.

9 OCTOBER: I'm standing just below Cotterstock lock, and there's what appears to be a kingfisher flying upstream towards me. At

least I think it's a kingfisher, but it seems very slow and there's something strange about its profile. Then I realise that it's carrying a large fish, a bullhead, by the tail. Its wings are whirring but making slow progress under the weight. It lands on a dead alder tree for a moment and shakes the fish about. It's looking to stun it and break the bones by bashing it against a branch, but maybe the branches aren't solid enough. It takes off again, sinking towards the water with its struggling prey before rising to disappear round the bend to search for a better perch.

10 OCTOBER: It's a fine day for the World Conker Championship, which is an endearingly daft competition started locally by a group of friends left with nothing to do after a cancelled fishing trip in the 1960s. It's grown into an annual event that attracts people from across the world. There's a great deal of fun and fancy dress, and a lot of money is raised for charity. It's happening just down the road in Southwick, so I go along to watch and lend support.

Each competitor draws a string with a horse chestnut threaded on to it from a bag. Then everyone is paired with another player, and each takes turns to try and smash the other's conker by taking a swing at it with their own. The winner goes on to the next round, drawing a new conker each time, until there are only two people left in the final. The victor is crowned champion.

After watching the first round of competitors battling it out in the pub garden, I walk past the church and carry on up the hill towards the forest. I sit on a bench and look back down into the valley. The pub's hidden by trees, but I can hear applause and laughter and the faint strum of a ukulele band. I concentrate on the natural sounds around me. On the left, three ravens come flying in with their croaking calls and settle on fence posts. Somewhere to the right a red kite gives a high, thin cry. A great spotted woodpecker *chikk*s in the trees behind.

I feel in my pocket for a conker I'd picked up in the village and take it out. It's about an inch and a half in diameter, and feels as hefty as a pebble. It has the rich brown colour of polished walnut furniture. The surface is hard and shiny. Digging a thumbnail into it leaves no impression. Distorted reflections of my face move around on its shiny surface as I rotate my hand.

During World War I, schoolchildren were asked to collect large amounts of conkers and acorns for what was officially described as "invaluable war work". They provided a homegrown source of starch which was converted into acetone, a vital ingredient in the manufacture of cordite for shells and bullets. I imagine the children in the village gathering them into sacks to be carted off to the railway station and delivered to a factory for processing.

I'm jolted back into the present as a group of Civil War re-enactors on the cricket pitch next to the pub fires a volley of muskets into the air. Smoke rises as the sound rolls along the valley, and rooks explode from the vicarage treetops in a great cawing spin. I walk back down to the village. There's a lingering smell of gunpowder as morris dancers clack and jingle on the gravel car park.

The conker tournament is hotting up. A red-coated Chelsea pensioner stands on a dais playing conkers against a young man dressed as a Cavalier. The pensioner wins. The crowd goes wild. There are many more games to be played before there's an overall winner, but in 2017 one of his colleagues was crowned world conker champion at the tender age of eighty-five.

11 OCTOBER: I've never visited John Clare's cottage in Helpston, so decide to drive to Wansford and walk the last seven miles to his home village through the landscape he knew so well. I park by the old station and cross the River Nene using the railway bridge. The path runs next to the tracks, and there are bright blue harebells on the embankment and a sharp smell of soot. It then follows the river before running through large sheep fields that mark the site of the Roman pottery town of Durobrivae.

I walk through Ailsworth and take the road to Helpston. It rises uphill into open countryside as the traffic falls away. The sun's out, and leaves are showing the bright reds and yellows of autumn. A skylark sings as a kestrel skims down a sloping field and turns into the wind to hover. The roadside hedges have recently been cut. In places the cutter has missed the wispy, climbing trails of old man's beard.

To the left of the road lie the oak and ash woods of Castor Hanglands. Further to the west there's a nature reserve that's open to all, but KEEP OUT signs assert that this part belongs to Milton Estates. Clare had many dealings with the estate throughout his life. He was totally opposed to the enclosures that stopped him walking in the places where he grew up. I can imagine his response to the sign. A robin sings defiantly from deep within the trees.

A few miles further on, the oaks and ashes at the side of the road give way to a beech wood, and there are different dappled shadows on the road. I walk through the trees to feel the snap and crackle of dry leaves underfoot. After that the road descends toward Helpston, which Clare described as "a gloomy village in Northamptonshire, on the brink of the Lincolnshire fens." To the east there are flat sea-level fields. They stretch to a horizon that could well be the world's edge.

In the village there's the cheerful sound of children playing at the village primary school, then the sudden rush of a high-speed train passing on the East Coast Main Line. Clare watched the surveyors plan the original line and lamented the way it split the landscape. The only time he travelled by train was when his coffin was brought back home from Northampton after his death in 1864. Clare Cottage is a thatched stone building on the main street, within sight of the church and right by the Bluebell Inn. It's owned by the John Clare Trust and maintained as a museum of the poet's life.

It's quite large and light inside, the sort of house that might now be owned by a city banker commuting to London. It takes a lot of imagination to picture the true state of the three small rooms at one end where Clare was born and later lived with his wife and seven children. Some of his possessions are on display, and I'm fascinated by a beautifully copied-out book of music and songs that he played on his violin. Many were learnt from local gypsies.

There are displays about the landowners' enclosures that separated Clare and his fellow villagers from their traditional haunts and grazing lands. A chalkboard invites visitors to add comments. Someone has written: "Privatisation is the new enclosures!" After reading about the mental struggles that dogged his later life I leave the main building and go out into the dovehouse. A film display shows different faces and voices, young and old, reading his great and harrowing poem *I Am*. It was written far from home in Northampton asylum, and the depressed and hopeless line "I am the self-consumer of my woes" hits me like a punch in the gut.

In the garden there's a scent of honeysuckle. Sparrows squabble in a hedge. I walk up to the nearby church to visit Clare's grave. He's described on the stone as The Northamptonshire Peasant Poet. That's how he was known when his poetry was first introduced to the world. He was a sensation for a while, but the reading public moved on, and he ended up back in poverty and ill health. It took a long time for his true worth as a poet to be appreciated. In 1989 a plaque was unveiled commemorating Clare in Poet's Corner in Westminster Abbey. The inscription there includes his own words: "Fields were the essence of the song". That echoes his own explanation for where he found the inspiration for his poems: "I kicked them from the clods while ploughing in the fields".

As I walk back through the village and up the hill towards home there's the quiet sound of blackbirds practising their song in the bushes. Further along the road a sparrowhawk swoops down on a wood pigeon at the edge of a copse. As I come down the hill into Ailsworth, a thatcher climbs a ladder propped up against the roof of an old stone cottage. Tucked under his left arm is a large, lifelike and beautifully crafted straw sculpture of a running hare.

16 OCTOBER: There's a kingfisher by the bridge this morning. It soon flies off, but I spot it again further downstream, perched on a hawthorn in the full light of the sun. Its feathers are as fresh and bright as any I've seen. A swan preens itself among the leafy fronds of a weeping willow nearby. Sunbeams bounce off the water's surface and chase across the pure white of its head and breast.

At Cotterstock, a pair of grey wagtails fly round and round, starting at the bridge, then across the pond to the miller's house, then onto the roof of the mill itself, then back down to where they started. One dislodges a piece of moss from the mill roof, which rolls down the old stone slates and tumbles towards the mill stream. The bird flits back to the bridge before the moss even hits the water. As I walk by the church there are villagers at the roadside planting daffodil bulbs for next spring.

When I get to the wood there's the loud alarm call of a robin coming from high in the trees. Further down the path there's the chatter of a magpie, then an unexpected black and white shape on the path. It's a dead badger, lying among the fallen leaves. Its head faces up the slope with the chin on the ground and the front paws reaching out on either side. The powerful front claws are open as if clinging to the earth. The back legs are hidden under the body. The white stripe down the centre of its head is clean and bright. So are the ear tufts. A single ash key has landed on its back. There's no sign of a struggle or disease, and no smell of decay. A dog comes bounding up, far away from its owners, and for an awful moment I think it might interfere with the corpse. But it just has a good look, takes a few sniffs at the head, then bounds off again.

I notice that the leaves have been disturbed nearby, and there are hanks of white hair scattered about. I follow their trail a short way up the slope and find a badger sett among the roots of an alder tree. The animals are known to be hygienic, and it could be that it died there and was dragged away by its peers. Why it died is a mystery but at least I'm beginning to get some idea of why it might have ended up where it is.

18 OCTOBER: I walk up the sloping track from Southwick. It's late afternoon, and the sky above the treeline is eggshell-blue smudged with wisps of grey charcoal. There's a sudden bellow

from deep in the forest: the guttural belch of a rutting fallow deer. As I walk along a woodland ride a group of hinds gathers in the distance. They turn and look over their shoulders at me but don't seem alarmed. The stag sounds to be less than a hundred yards away so I stop. I don't often feel vulnerable in the English countryside, but deer can be a danger to humans during the mating season. This feels close enough.

The stag falls quiet as dusk closes in. An owl calls and a goldcrest tinkles. Squirrels chunter and scamper through the branches. A jay screeches. There's a smell of cold, damp earth. Then a muntjac deer barks and some cattle start to low in the fields beyond. The fallow stag resumes his deep, grunting calls. 🔊 10.39

Later, there are sounds like twigs and branches being banged together. The stag could be butting the trees or locking antlers with a rival. Hairs rise on the back of my neck. It's time to go.

I walk back along the track as the sounds begin to fade. These woodlands were part of the old Rockingham Forest, a favourite royal hunting ground. Fallow deer were brought here by the Normans, so this ritual roaring, fighting and breeding has been going on for a very long time. As I get to the edge of the trees, I remember starting down the path towards Southwick on a night just like this one. I was brought to a sudden halt by the profile of an antlered stag standing with its hinds about thirty yards ahead. It turned straight towards me and hurled a loud bark that was as startling as a gunshot. The trees were a long way behind me, and running seemed a bad idea. Blind instinct took over. I froze, not breathing, arms held rigidly at my sides and shoulders drawn up towards my ears in a bid to look as thin and insignificant as possible. The stag didn't move. Then it slowly swung its head to one side and took off across the field with its hinds following. The thud of their hooves came up through the ground, mingling with the thump of my relieved and grateful heartbeats.

20 OCTOBER: It's too wet to walk first thing this morning. Instead, I sit for a while in a shell-shaped chair in the conservatory with my eyes closed. The rain starts as a steady roar of applause then gradually breaks into individual handclaps. Different sounds roll across. Dry crackles of burning brushwood. The fizz of fireworks. Soft radio static. Sometimes there's no obvious rhythm. At other times horses gallop by and trains rattle along a rickety track.

I once sat here with my harp while gentle rain was beating out a 'one two three, one two three, one two...' rhythm. I picked out some repeating notes from that pattern, creating a melody and harmony to fit around them. Later, when I was playing the tune in a care home, I explained to the residents how I'd come to write it. One of them told me afterwards that it took her right back to the sound of the rain on the tin roofs of her African childhood.

The rain on the roof fades to a gentle patter and I set out for a walk. There are bright, wet leaves on the dark tarmac road. When I get to the wood, they're sprawled like spillikins across the woodland floor. Most have fallen from ash trees with their pinnate pairs of leaves set opposite each other on the stem, but there are also oak, beech and willow. Their warm colours soften the path and nestle among the trees like scattered flowers. As they fall, they let in more light from above. They also reflect it back up again. The wood's lit up like a second spring.

Lines and shapes have softened, and the path is drier and less muddy. I come to the water's edge. Leaves have settled on the surface. They're so packed that I'm almost tempted to walk on them. Further down the track the sweet smell of bruised leaves gives way to something different. The dead badger's still near the path, but on each successive day it's been dragged a few more yards down the slope. There are new tufts of hair lying about. I think badgers are moving it at night. There are still no marks on the body, but it's beginning to smell a little so I'm less inclined to stop and hang around.

21 OCTOBER: The river level's up and the wind's shifted to the west. Gulls settle in puddles and a lone magpie perches on a sheep's back. By the time I'm level with the wood the tall ash trees give shelter to the yellowing willows at the river's edge and the water's dead flat. Yesterday the leaves were falling and settling like snow. Today there's hardly a leaf out of place.

Beyond the weir a kestrel is being chased by crows. It wheels round and round and up and down, but they stick to its tail and force it past the trees into the blue sky beyond. I'm startled by a braying honk from above: cormorants. When they arrive here in numbers it's a proper sign of the coming winter. There are four in their new tree, perched on an upturned lightning strike of dead and broken branches. Their black wing feathers gleam in the morning light. By the lock a kingfisher hovers above the far bank. It heads off upstream and clings for the brief moment to a swaying reed stalk before flying off into the distance.

When I get to the wood I look out for the badger. It's much further down the slope now, hidden under some branches. The body's on its back. The ribs have been stripped clean and the body cavity's empty. It could have been eaten by a fox, but I'm beginning to wonder if there's been some cannibalism going on. It's a taboo for humans but not unknown in many species of animals.

24 OCTOBER: This morning there is a lot of excitable behaviour from birds on the path back from Cotterstock. As I walk through the village I can already hear skylarks in the fields. When I get there, I find a gap in the hedge and watch. To start with there is just one bird singing from the ground, then half a dozen skylarks lift off in pairs and start buzzing one other. After that they fly low across the field and hover. During all this time they are spitting out notes like sparks. Then they come back down to earth and sit in silence until one begins to sing, which sets the whole cycle off again.

As I walk further along the hedgerow a flurry of yellow-feathered wings takes off and loops over to the far side. At first, I think it's goldfinches, then realise it's a flock of yellowhammers. They settle in the willow trees along the brook, barely visible among the yellowing autumn leaves.

25 OCTOBER: Walking towards the weir, I can hear a trilling from the far bank that can only be from a kingfisher. But it's unusually bright and varied. There could be another somewhere nearby. In the willows I can see a patch of blue, then the leaves bob in the breeze and I can just make out another. The kingfishers are perched about a foot apart, and as they turn to look across the river their breast feathers show bright orange.

They're sitting still and quiet. Sometimes the one on the left lengthens its body upwards and turns as if to bow towards the other. It's very moving to see them so comfortable together. They stay like this for about ten minutes, then a posse of long-tailed tits passes through the trees behind them and they take off. One flies in a slower and more deliberate way than the other and lets out a long, soft trill.

Further down the bank a flock of about a dozen goldfinches gleams red and yellow among the teasels. They take off as I get close, and fly in a twittering ball across the meadows.

26 OCTOBER: I'm standing on the bridge looking into the millpond. My ears home in on the sounds. There are low bubbles and burbles, and the swish and lap of broken water. I'm starting to feel transported. In the words of the nineteenth-century nature writer and mystic Richard Jeffries, this is "a pool to stand near and think into".

Fallen leaves are being pushed deep below the surface by the force of the water coming under the bridge. Then they start to swim up again in slow wavy patterns. There are yellow willows, green ash, red sycamores and copper beech. All meet, separate and spin in a stately dance. Each one is a memory of spring and summer, of life and growth created by soil, sun and water. I'm looking into a crystal ball that never repeats, never shows the same thing twice. The leaves could be stars, or words, or worlds.

30 OCTOBER: I'm walking by the river at sundown on the last day before the clocks change for winter. The path's slippery, and I slow down and stop for a moment. It's very still. The cool air smells of rain. The sky's a colour wash of pink, orange and turquoise. Rooks circle and caw. A pheasant whirrs its wings. Blackbirds chink in the hawthorns. As I turn for home the last lights in the sky reflect off the smooth, bowed surface of the river. At the centre they're blue and grey, brightening to white and gold at the edges.

31 OCTOBER: Yesterday evening was the calm before an almighty storm. Waking to the sound of steady rain and gusty winds, I decide to stay indoors till it clears. The weather forecast is for winds of twenty miles per hour, but this is much wilder. I pop my head out of the back door. The drenching rain is horizontal, and trees are being wrenched about in all directions. The wind rises to a shriek. I've only heard that note once before, during a near-hurricane in the Lincolnshire Fens. There's going to be a lot of damage.

Luckily the worst is soon over. It blows itself out after about twenty minutes and the sky clears. I look up the readings from the local weather station. The strongest gusts had been close to seventy miles per hour. That qualifies as a violent storm, force eleven. I set off for a walk, feeling slightly giddy. The ground's full of the drips and trickles of running water. The air smells clean. There are small twigs and branches on the path to the bridge. I have to skip over puddles caused by leaf-clogged drains.

As I walk down the far side of the river, a bright sun comes out. Looking across, I can see the trees in the wood have been affected. The willows look thin, more like etchings than oil paintings. A lot of branches have come down, and the big willow with the fungus has split its trunk and fallen right along the bank.

I turn back thinking about Halloween. In the Celtic tradition it's known as Samhain. It starts this evening and goes on till tomorrow. Like May Day it's one of the two 'hinges of the year', turning points between summer and winter. It's thought of as a time when this life and the afterlife are at their closest. This morning certainly feels like the preparation for a shift of perception.

In the evening I feel drawn to the badgers. When I get to the entrance to the wood there's a tangle of fallen trunks and branches blocking the path. I walk along the edge of the trees in the darkness and find a gap where I can get near to the sett. I try to stay upwind so they won't catch my scent, but the breeze is swirling around and it's pointless. I sit on a fallen trunk listening to the darkened wood. It's been a bruising day but the swish in the trees feels gentler now.

A flickering blue light spills into the wood from the bypass, strobing across the tree trunks. An emergency vehicle starts up its siren. A fox lets out a sudden unearthly wail that's perfectly in tune with it, sending a shiver down my back. I leave the wood and walk back into town. Doors and windows are decorated with plastic skeletons and grinning pumpkins. Children dressed as ghouls squeal in excitement as they trot along the pavements clutching bags of sweets. Their bed-sheet shrouds and painted faces are lit up by the ghostly glare of their parents' phone torches.

NOVEMBER

All Saints' Day   Red kites   Wren   Birdsong memories
King Alfred's cakes   Craft fair   Remembrance Day   Carp
Starlings   Listening to the wind   A fox in the frost
Whooper swans

1 NOVEMBER: It's All Saints' Day, my birthday. Both call for celebration, but at the back of my mind I'm apprehensive about the scale of the damage in the wood. When I arrive there it's clear that the ash trees at the top of the slope have suffered the worst. They took the full force of the southwest wind while still carrying most of their autumn leaves. Several have keeled over like tall ships under full sail. Trunks and boughs have snapped, and wreckage is piled up high above my head. I have to dive, duck and climb to get through.

As I go further into the wood a thick layer of leaves and twigs swishes and scrunches underfoot. The trees here have fared better. I head down towards the river edge to check on my favourite ash, the one with the long horizontal branch. It's fine, but a smaller neighbour has fallen against it. I try to think of some positives. There's more light coming through the canopy which should prompt regeneration, and the dead wood created will benefit both beetles and woodpeckers. There are also plenty of potential new kingfisher perches on the fallen trees by the river. Otherwise it feels like a scene of devastation.

2 NOVEMBER: The wind drops and the warmth of the sun comes through. Clouds of gnats dance in the sunshine and gossamer spiders drift on an imperceptible breeze. Skylarks sing above the fields. Across the countryside people are clearing up after the storm. There's a treacly smell of damp bonfires. A convoy of vans towing woodchippers speeds by on its way to fix broken power lines.

On the way back from Cotterstock, there's a mysterious crunching sound on the other side of a tall hedgerow. When I come to a gap in the hedge, I can see that it's a line of sheep. They're keeping pace with me as they follow one another through a thick carpet of dry, fallen leaves.

4 NOVEMBER: I'm walking up to the forest from Southwick with a strong southerly wind at my back. It's been a bright day with sudden squalls of rain. A young fallow deer stops and stares from a field as I pass. Later it appears again from the trees and crosses the path in front of me. Bright red and gold bramble leaves stand out against the green at the edge of the ride. Russet-coloured ferns stretch away into a clearing. A goldcrest flits unseen among the branches. Its non-stop chitter is as bright and tiny as the bird itself.

I get to the far end of the path through the trees and stop. It's an hour from sunset. The sun's low on my left and restless black cloudlets race across a turquoise sky like a speeded-up video. Open ploughed fields sweep up in front of me. There's a herd of deer by a group of trees on the horizon. Heads turn, and a row of ears bobs along the upper border of their shadowy silhouette. I take the path to the east along the edge of the forest. It's sheltered here, and warmer, but I can still hear the wind roaring above the trees. Ahead of me a kettle of red kites floats and spins like tea leaves in a swirling sky.

When I get closer, I count twenty or more sailing in a hundred-yard circle. They're facing into the wind, hanging in the air with lazy wing flaps and trims and tweaks of their forked tails. As they glide above me, light shows through the open fingers of their wingtip feathers. Sometimes they peel away on a slow sally downwind then return again. One might shadow another, but there's no pattern, no plan. There's just an easy rhythm, bonded together like a shared dream. I step up onto a stile, eager to be off the ground, closer to the sky. I stop wondering what they're doing, and just wonder. They are souls, spirits, and they know I'm here.

The last of the sun breaks through from the west and there's rain in the wind. To the east is low-lit cloud with the tint and texture of a Turner painting. The end of a rainbow flares up from a skeletal ash grove, two wide rows of pink and turquoise that focus into the full spectrum of colours then dissolve again. The kites are still there in the sky, gently falling with a dip of one shoulder then rising up again. Pigeons dash across, and a shape-shifting flock of starlings homes in on its roost. There's the first questioning call of a tawny owl from the woods behind, and the harsh bark of a raven.

I climb down from the stile and stumble back through the forest, up the muddy slope and past the remains of an overgrown wooden railway carriage that was once lived in by a tramp. By the edge of the trees above Southwick a kestrel drifts in the last of the light. Further up the valley, black sheets of rain hang from an oncoming squall. I shelter in the lee of an oak tree and lean back against it with the trunk between my shoulder blades. It's firm and warm through my jacket, and starts to vibrate as the rain thrums against its leaves and the wind gusts through the branches. I begin to lose sense of where the tree ends and my body begins.

I've been flying with the kites, but now I'm grounding again. My feet are rooting in the earth.

The weather lifts and I set off downhill in the dark. I can only see a short section of the path in front of me, but I know that it heads into the valley in a dead straight line. As I look along it, then look up, there's a mist-haloed half-moon hovering over the looming shape of Southwick Hill.

5 NOVEMBER: Reflecting on watching the red kites, I realise that such a thing would have been impossible when I first moved to the area. Red kites have become a common sight in local skies but there was a long period when there were none. Persecution by gamekeepers and egg collectors caused them to die out in the UK during the nineteenth century, and they dwindled to just a few pairs left in Wales. A project to reintroduce them in the Chilterns started in 1990 using birds imported from Spain. That worked so well that, in 1995, birds were also released in Fineshade Wood, to the northwest of Oundle. They've greatly enriched the life and colour of the local landscape, and have bred so well that some have recently been sent back to Spain to help with conservation programmes where local populations of red kites have plummeted.

6 NOVEMBER: This has been one of those days when you set out for a walk in one season and return in another. First there was a chill mist with nothing much to see but dew on the cobwebs and gossamer trails on the wet grass. Then the sun broke through. A grey heron stood on a bare branch and held its wings out to the warmth. Birds sang, insects swarmed. I looked up at the sky through golden beech leaves till the world started spinning.

When I got home there were some emails from people looking for birdsong recordings. One was from a music recording studio wanting to use natural sounds in the introduction to a song. The other was from a bereaved family planning to play the sound of a blackbird during their relative's funeral service. They were a reminder of just how special these sounds can be at a time when people are turning to music and poetry to express their shared memories and feelings.

I once had an urgent request from a hospice whose staff had been frantically searching for a recording of a nightingale for a dying patient who regretted never hearing one. There was no time to lose, and my hands were shaking as I searched for the right files and sent them off in an email. A few minutes later they came back to say that the wards were full of birdsong. Another time I got a message from a family saying that they played one of my recordings to a dying relative who had listened to nightingales every spring near his tiny village in the south of England. The family were gathered round his bed, and he seemed completely unconscious. But everyone present was convinced that he was listening once more.

7 NOVEMBER: I'm looking down from the bridge at the edge of the millpond and there's a large clump of reeds in the still waters at its edge. They've grown up to eight feet tall over the summer, with closely packed round stems that are an inch wide at water level and taper to a sharp tip. A few are still green, but most vary in colour from freckled russet to light grey and yellow straw. Some are bent and broken about halfway up and have folded across to form a deep lattice of overlapping angular shapes: triangles, rhombi and pentangles.

I can hear the loud, sharp chitter of a wren but can't see it. Then I start to spot parts of its body through the stems as it moves rapidly about: an eye, a beak, then a chestnut tail. It's foraging for insects, hiding and perching for split seconds at a time. Eventually the wren emerges, framed in a perfect parallelogram of reeds. Its feet grip the roundness of a horizontal stem as the beak points down and the tail cocks skywards.

On the way back home I take the path through the woods by the river. There's a kingfisher call just ahead. I move forward carefully, hardly daring to breathe. It's in a willow about twenty feet away. This time last week the leaves would have masked it but now I can see clearly. It's a male, the first I've seen in a long time. The orange breast glows against the bare dark twigs around it. It looks into the water for a moment then suddenly thrusts into the air and speeds off upriver.

9 NOVEMBER: This whole kingfisher experience seems to be reaching another level. I set out to walk round Snipe Meadow at about 4.40pm when the light is fading. When I get to the cut by the bridge, I realise that I've never worked out where the local kingfishers spend the night. They're known to roost on a hidden branch with one wing pulled over their head.

Then I notice one about thirty feet away on the far bank. It is sitting on a willow branch at about head height. The light is so gloomy that only the white of its ruff and dim glow of its breast feathers give it away. There is no light left for fishing by now, but it isn't ready to settle down, and eventually flies off towards the main river. As I carry on along the riverside path it calls and passes twice before perching for a few seconds on a swaying reed just in front of me. I look across at the big yellow full moon rising in the east and have to wonder: who is watching whom?

The more I watch and listen to nature the more I'm inclined towards animism, the feeling that all natural things have souls. That's very much against scientific thinking, and there's a danger of tipping over into believing that animals and birds might have human traits and characteristics. But it's a thread that runs through a lot of nature writing. I remember reading *The Wind in the Willows* as a child and getting a strange feeling when I got to the chapter called 'The Piper at the Gates of Dawn'. It no longer seemed like a children's book. There's a strong current of paganism in the story as Mole and Rat get closer to Pan. Rat seems to enter a trance and whispers: "This is the place of my song-dream, the place the music played to me". Those words send a shiver down my back even now. Perhaps that's what I'm looking and listening for by the river, the place of my song-dream.

10 NOVEMBER: I seem to discover a different type of fungus in the wood every day. This morning I spot some intriguing round black lumps the size and colour of squash balls on the fallen trunk of an ash tree. I bring a couple home. When I look them up I find out they're called 'King Alfred's cakes'. The name refers to a story I remember being told at school about King Alfred hiding in a peasant couple's home after a defeat by the Danes in AD878. The wife didn't know who Alfred was and asked him to watch some cakes baking over a fire while she went outside to do an errand. He forgot all about the cakes and burned them. She quite rightly scolded him when she came back.

I think the point of this story was that Alfred was so gracious that he just accepted the telling-off, rather than inform her who he was and that he had more weighty matters on his mind. But even as an eight-year-old I thought it said more about how useless we can be at concentrating on tasks that don't interest us.

I get out the two pieces of fungus to look at them. They look and feel like charcoal. There is a sharp, hollow sound when I tap them with a fingernail. King Alfred fungus has been used since Neolithic times to help light and maintain fires. It acts as tinder to convert a spark into a flame and glows long enough to be a means of transferring fire from one place to another.

I put one on a square of thick cardboard on the conservatory table and hold a match to it. Even though it has just been taken from a damp wood, it starts to glow straight away. It gives off a thin trail of smoke like a joss stick. I stub it out with my finger then go off to do other things around the house. Ten minutes later I hear the fire alarm and rush back to find the conservatory full of smoke. There is nothing left of the fungus, and the cardboard has almost burnt through to the tabletop.

Alfred managed to burn the cakes. I could have burnt the conservatory. Luckily no one is around to tell me off for being so daft. But it's a good lesson that even the tiniest source of fire can be dangerous, and an impressive demonstration of an unlikely traditional use for a fungus.

12 NOVEMBER: This morning I'm playing the harp at a Christmas craft fair in St Peter's church. It's something I do every year. The church is a lovely warm building with a fine acoustic, and the event gives me a chance to meet old friends. When I'm playing background music it's always interesting to see the ways in which different people react. Some walk by without a second glance,

others stop and listen. They're often parents with young children. I can see them pointing towards the strings and explaining how my fingers move to create the sound. Sometimes I'll switch to a simple song such as *Twinkle Twinkle Little Star* to draw them in still further.

Today I am concentrating on a difficult new tune and become aware that someone has stopped close by. When I look up, it's Emmi. I met her earlier in the year when she was walking by the river with her husband Chris and their baby daughter Robyn. At the time Robyn was asleep in a sling, but now she is wide awake and looking at me. I watch her eyes as I play. They look towards my moving fingers then gently up in the air and from side to side before coming back to the harp. She appears fascinated. It looks like there's some real listening going on.

My mind makes a sudden jump to the tiny kingfisher chick I'd seen back in July. I think of the way it slowly looked around and reacted to the birds singing in the trees overhead. There's the same sense of a shiny new soul taking in the shapes, sounds and colours of the world. It's a lovely moment.

13 NOVEMBER: This afternoon Oundle holds its Remembrance Day parade. It is poignant to watch local school pupils dressed in military uniform, honouring the deaths of soldiers who were not much older than them when they set off to war. My dad's father, who died long before I was born, was a tank driver in World War I. It's hard to imagine the noise, heat, fear and fumes he endured in what was then a totally new form of warfare. At the same time my great-uncle Gerald left his life working as a groom at the manor house in his home village in Dorset to tend to horses being used

at the Battle of the Somme. I often wonder whether he heard nightingales while he was there, and saw other birds, trees and flowers that reminded him of home. He didn't come back. The family got an official notification that he was missing in action, and his body was never found.

I am still thinking about my grandfather and great-uncle in the evening, when a gale starts to blow. I set off along the path to the wood, struggling against the wind in the dark, and step in among the fallen trunks. It is as if the surviving trees are holding a requiem, their ivy-festooned branches twisting and thrumming like tuning forks against a dark purple sky. There are sounds like crashing waves, waterfalls and the thunder of falling rocks. There are noises of war too: the drone of a helicopter, clashing anvils and gunfire. Then the wind adds a long, low mournful groan like a bass chord from a Russian choir. The note rises and rises till it can stand no more. Then it falls back to earth with an exhausted, plaintive sigh.

15 NOVEMBER: It's wonderfully still by the river this morning. You can't tell the trees apart from their reverse images in the water until rising fish ripples start pixelating their reflections. Gossamer spiders are out in force, tickling my cheeks and eyebrows. A pair attach themselves to the peak of my cap and abseil in front of my nose.

The traffic on the road sounds like distant surf. I can hear the whirr of small birds flitting through the trees on the far bank, and the thin chatter of falling leaves pinballing down through the branches to the forest floor. I stop at the weir and take in the peppermint-and-fresh-cream scent of breaking water. I can just hear a kingfisher upstream, but for once am too busy taking in what is right in front of me. Two wrens rattle away at each other in the undergrowth. Then the whole scene starts to glow with the light, and I turn to gaze up at a bright sun emerging from a cloudy weather front into a half-sky of pure blue.

A big military plane drones overhead. It reminds me how lucky I am to be in this safe and peaceful space. A kestrel flies by with its rapid wingbeats and perches high in a tree to the right. I watch as it scans the ground for food. Then there is a mewl from another kestrel across the meadows, and it stiffens and takes off. I walk on to the lock and just manage to see the back end of a kingfisher disappearing up the cut. A song thrush is singing its heart out for a few moments by the pond, the first I've heard since the summer.

This is a special day, and I know it. I take a long, slow saunter back along the river and walk up onto the bridge. The aroma from the restaurant at the wharf means it must be midday at least. I've completely lost track. A female kingfisher is sitting quietly among the thorny branches by the boathouse. Her beak tilts down towards the water. I watch until a dog walker comes along, and she breaks cover and whizzes off under the bridge. A special day indeed.

16 NOVEMBER: As I walk along the path towards upper Barnwell lock there's a mistle thrush singing on the far side of a lake. It's calling from an area that's beautifully fringed with trees and reeds. I'm drawn towards it, but on the way round I spot something lying on a low horizontal branch by the water. It's a dead carp over two feet long, a silvery white shape against the green bark, yellow leaves and orange fungus.

It's the sort of trophy fish you'd normally see being held up to the camera by a grinning angler. I suspect this one's been killed by an otter. The head and tail are still there but some flesh has been stripped from the bones and ribs in the middle. It must have put up quite a struggle. Scales are scattered around like blood-spotted confetti. I pick one up. It's translucent, like thin mother-of-pearl. I hold it to the light and can see the pink flesh of my finger through it. It's etched with concentric circles like a fingerprint, or the growth rings of a tree. As I leave, the mistle thrush starts to sing again. Of all birds it makes the perfect soundtrack. Eerie, unworldly and strangely beautiful.

18 NOVEMBER: I drive before dusk to Titchmarsh nature reserve, hoping for a repeat of the spectacular starling murmurations that swirled across the sky last year. They haven't started yet, but big flocks of jackdaws are arriving from all points of the compass. They flap about in groups before settling in their thousands in the trees on the far side of the water. Their constant, machine-like cawing and clacking threatens to drown out the goose honks and wigeon whistles from the middle of the lake. A great white egret wings silently across the water.

I choose a spot with an uninterrupted view of the lake and sky and wait. As the sun gets lower the few feathery clouds glow, and the sky turns pink and gold. Starlings fly across in small numbers to begin with, then quickly gather into larger groups. Others come streaming across the muddy fields till there are three or four separate flocks of thousands swaying across the sky. One comes directly overhead with an alternating rhythm of quick, coordinated wingbeats and short glides. Each bird is flying relatively slowly but the overall effect is of swift, graceful movements.

As each group turns to fly away the texture becomes thinner, then thicker again as it comes broadside on. Sometimes flocks appear to pulse like a beating heart as they cross one other and make swaying, balletic shapes in the sky. The birds start to peel away and rain straight down into reed beds to disappear from sight. I can hear hundreds of voices as they jostle for position among the stalks. Flying close to one of the flocks is a single sparrowhawk. One of the reasons for these spectacular displays is that the large numbers and movements of the birds confuses predators. The hawk follows the starlings down to the beds and flies back and forth above them. They are just feet away, but the hawk never seems to make a kill.

When the starlings have all roosted I set off back in the gathering darkness. A barn owl flies down the path with its round face coming straight at me. It veers off to the left at the last moment. It looks startlingly large and white against the gloom, but is completely silent as its powerful wings beat the air on the way past.

20 NOVEMBER: While walking the riverbank this morning I look up to watch a skein of greylag geese pass overhead. At the same time I am taking in gulls and cormorants flying at different heights and angles, plus the ducks and swans on the water. I'm suddenly transported into a poster of waterbirds that was on our primary school classroom wall in the 1960s. I can smell the chalky blackboards and dry powder paint.

After an extended mild autumn it feels like winter has arrived. There are patches of frost on the path as I walk into a steady north wind. Two flocks of fieldfares scoot over, heading south, and some redwings perch in the trees by the bridge. The reeds in the pond have collapsed into a shapeless tangle of ancient thatch. On a dull day the colour looks to be leaching out of the landscape, but this morning's bright sun picks out the sparse gold leaves left on the willows. In Cotterstock, beech leaves are piled up between black painted railings like glowing orange embers.

24 NOVEMBER: I don't often talk to trees, but I listen to them a lot. Today a southerly wind blows through the bare branches of the first willow down from the bridge. I stand there for a few minutes. There are no rustles, just a soft moan or drone, more distant seashore than riverbank.

I walk on to Cotterstock, and the horse chestnuts by the hall have a deeper, darker tone that rises and falls, fading to silence then picking up again. The ashes in the wood have a disturbingly deep bass undertone when the wind roars, but today all I can hear is a high, rain-like splashing sound coming from the rippling ivy leaves as they flap about among the trunks and branches.

26 NOVEMBER: As I walk onto the bridge this morning there are some loud and scratchy kingfisher calls coming from the bushes on the other side of the cut. I can't see anything to begin with, but then a bird flies from right beneath me and lands in a willow tree on the far side. If I had thought to look over the stone parapet it would have been perched about ten feet below where I am standing.

It flits between branches before settling low in the corner by the storm culvert. From there it does a series of dives into the water to bathe, returning each time to the same place to clean and preen its feathers. It draws its wings across the face and breast, then shakes its head and body from side to side. Then it crouches down, stretches forwards and flicks up its tail.

This is beginning to look like display behaviour, and at that moment another kingfisher comes flying in from the right. It does a tight circling turn before taking off towards the main river with the first bird in close pursuit. I watch them for as long as I can, but they are flying fast and aren't going to be landing anywhere near. This makes sense of the very loud calls I heard when I first arrived. They were amplified by being bounced off the stone of the bridge and the building next to it, and the kingfisher may have chosen to call from there for just that reason. Other species of birds routinely find the best positions to sing from so they can get their point across loud and clear. I haven't thought of kingfishers in that way before, but I will now.

28 NOVEMBER: It's a beautiful frosty morning. Song thrushes are singing along the river. A buzzard swoops low towards a hedgerow. Sheep are startled by starlings that flit among their legs in search of food.

On the far bank, there's an outpouring of fury from two wrens perched on a barbed-wire fence. Right by them is a fox sitting on its haunches. It's next to the entrance to its earth, and is facing me across the river with its eyes closed. Steam rises from its muzzle. It appears to be sunning itself. The wrens are still rattling away, but otherwise it's a scene of complete relaxation. I watch for a few minutes, but have to get home soon, so cough politely to see if there's any response. The fox opens its eyes with what sounds like a snort of indignation. Then it glares across the water at me and slinks sullenly back into its earth. I feel a bit embarrassed about disturbing it, but at least its retreat gives the wrens a chance to get back to a quieter life.

30 NOVEMBER: A naturalist friend was telling me about the whooper swans that come to spend the winter at Welney Wetland Centre. He described how the birds arrive from Iceland after a flight of twelve hundred miles. Their breast feathers are stained by minerals in the water of the lakes where they spend their summers. I am keen to hear their distinctive honking call, so set off an hour before sunrise and drive through the darkened fens past Wisbech, Outwell and Upwell.

As I get closer to Welney the cloudy sky is beginning to lighten in the east. The first skeins of swans are already flying west towards the fields where they will feed during the day. I am passing from the Nene catchment into the Ouse Washes, which are allowed to flood in winter to help control the river. The area is naturally low-lying. At one dip in the road a ruler marks the depth of potential floodwaters. It rises to eight feet above the level of the tarmac.

I arrive at the centre before it opens but am immediately drawn to sounds from a small reed-lined lake tucked away behind it. Sheltering from the wind and rain behind a wicker-woven hide, there's time to listen to a varied soundscape of tufted ducks, geese and wigeon. Big flocks of lapwings fly overhead as the first knots of whooper swans start to appear. There is a whistle from a kingfisher, and a dark profile wings low across the grey surface of the water.

When the centre opens I cross the bridge over the road to get into the observation points overlooking the washes. There is a big expanse of water with large numbers of swans, geese and ducks swimming or flying across. I am thrilled to get a recording as a whooper swan flies past with its extraordinarily evocative trumpeting call. 🔊 11.40

After reading some information boards I realise that all this has a connection with the conservationist Sir Peter Scott. He set up the Wildfowl and Wetlands Trust in 1946 at Slimbridge on the River Severn. Welney was the Trust's second reserve, and was created in 1950. The organisation was unusual at the time because it encouraged people to visit and observe wildlife rather than keeping them away.

Driving home, feeling profoundly grateful that places like Welney exist, I start to think about Peter Scott and all that he did. His role in increasing public understanding of wildlife was huge. I remember his distinctive voice from television documentaries I watched as a child. In his formative years Scott also had deep connections with Oundle and the River Nene. It feels like the time has come to delve further into his life and work.

DECEMBER

1 DECEMBER: In March 1912 the explorer Captain Robert Falcon Scott wrote a moving letter to his wife Kathleen. It was addressed: "To my widow". He was the leader of a British expedition that had hoped to be first to the South Pole. They were successful in reaching it but discovered that a Norwegian expedition led by Roald Amundsen had got there before them. The journey back was difficult, and it became clear that Scott and his colleagues weren't going to survive. In part of the letter to his wife he talks about his hopes for their two-year-old son Peter: "Make the boy interested in natural history if you can, it is better than games – they encourage it at some schools". Twelve years later the school she chose for him was Oundle. It was well known at the time for its teaching of science, including natural sciences.

The young Peter Scott grew up to be extremely interested in natural history. He also inherited the talents of his mother, who was a well-known artist and sculptor. In his autobiography *The Eye of the Wind*, Scott describes life at Oundle School in the 1920s. The school regime was comparatively easy-going. He had enough leisure time to become a keen fisherman, and sometimes cast his line into the River Nene from the bridge.

Scott became aware of the "romance and mystery" of large birds like geese during birdwatching expeditions to flooded stretches of the river around Lilford. He did anatomical drawings of birds which were lodged at the Natural History Museum and, with two fellow schoolboys, co-wrote an illustrated book about birds. He also kept tame bats and raised three species of owlets. He found barn owls the most "difficult", tawnies the "nicest" and little owls the "fiercest".

Scott left school to study zoology at Cambridge but didn't enjoy academic life. Instead, he spent much of his time wildfowling in the marshes and fens of the area. His interest in birds gradually widened over many years until he eventually became more interested in conserving birds than shooting them. After leaving Cambridge he rented an abandoned lighthouse at Sutton Bridge by the mouth of the River Nene. He gathered wild geese in his own enclosures there and started to establish his career as a wildlife and landscape painter. It was there that Scott's life and work began to come into focus. He launched a career that affected the lives of countless others, and eventually helped found the World Wildlife Fund. Sir David Attenborough credits him with inspiring his own interest in nature, and described him as "the patron saint of conservation".

2 DECEMBER: I've been reading more about Peter Scott, and found a passage where he talks about his favourite bird sounds. He appreciated "soloists" like the nightingale, blackcap and curlew, but thought the greatest "chorus" was provided by geese. I hadn't really thought about it that way before, but have to agree that he

was right. A big flock of geese honking together is an extraordinary sound. I set out early this morning to try and record one. I drive to Stanwick Lakes, part of a complex of flooded gravel pits upstream from Thrapston that I walked through back in the heat of the summer. Today it's very cold indeed.

There are different stretches of water, and I spend a while finding the best places to record. Eventually I come away with sounds of greylag and Canada geese, mixed in with the evocative whistles of wigeon ducks. For me they stir up memories of wind, water and cold weather in wide-open spaces. It's part of the soundtrack of winter. 🔊 12.41

3 DECEMBER: Since January I've been a little nervous that kingfishers would disappear from the river before the end of my year of watching them. I needn't have worried. There have been very few days when I haven't seen or heard one, and there's no let-up now. This afternoon there's a kingfisher perched high up in a willow tree by the bridge.

It takes its time choosing a target, then bobs its head and dives almost vertically into the water. That allows it to reach further into the depths where the fish swim when it's colder. It misses the first time, but returns to its high perch and dives again. This time it emerges with a fish.

I marvel again at how little splash and sound the kingfisher makes when it hits the water. It folds its wings and stretches out its neck to be more streamlined, and the shape of the beak has evolved to create the minimum of the shock waves which fish use to detect danger. This gives the bird a split-second advantage in surprising its prey.

The design of the kingfisher's beak was used by Japanese engineers to create the nose cone for high-speed bullet trains. Early prototypes of the train were far too noisy when they entered and left tunnels. An inspired designer investigated how the kingfisher's beak managed to make so little sound and resistance when it went from air into water. The engineers copied its cross section, which is shaped like a curved, flattened diamond. It reduced the noise and pressure created by the trains as they emerged from tunnels, and also increased fuel efficiency.

4 DECEMBER: It's a rainy day so I set out waterproofed from head to toe. I'm not expecting to see much by the river, but I'm wrong. Large, sleety raindrops hit the surface near the boathouse and send up little spouts of water into the air. In the distance an egret flies lazily round the bend in the river till it's lost in the rain and trees. At the millpond a sparrowhawk blurs past. A gaggle of fieldfares shoots straight up in the air as if they've been fired from a glitter cannon. They instantly scatter far and wide.

Best of all, I get to watch a wren. I hear the rattling song of our commonest bird every day, but it's rare to get more than a glimpse of it. I chance on one on a crinkly-leaved stalk by the bank. It's no more than ten feet away with just the rain-pocked river surface behind it. Despite the proximity, it doesn't notice me. It's tiny, with feathers in many delicate shades of brown. It looks beautifully balanced, perched on a diagonal, with its quick head movements and its cocked tail.

Then it takes off across the river using just enough wing power to get to the far side. There's a thin burst of song from low in the reeds and it's invisible once more.

5 DECEMBER: I'm walking by the river on the path opposite the wood and start to get the feeling that something's wrong. I've passed the dead tree where the kingfishers perch, and the burdock stalks where the goldfinches flit. By now I should be hearing water gushing over the weir, but there is only silence. When I get there the channel is dry. The water's flat and still in the stream below it.

Other walkers stop to look. They tell me men are working on the sluice at the mill race. They've opened it up to let more water through and that's made the river level fall. We gaze down at the dark green moss on the bed where the water normally flows. This scene is usually full of the sight and sound of rushing water. It concentrates and narrows the senses. Now the whole space feels wider and calmer. It's as strange and different as a landscape covered in snow.

It makes me realise how much sounds change our perception of a place. If we're expecting to hear a certain type and level of noise then any marked change means we have to reappraise the whole experience. It's also a reminder that rivers are fragile. If the water stops flowing then all that's left is a scar in the terrain. Flora and fauna evolve to depend on the ebb and flow of water through the seasons. If there's no water there are no aquatic plants, fish or insects.

Today the workmen have temporarily altered the flow to do maintenance, but all over the world permanent changes are happening because of commercial exploitation or climate change. If you live by a river or lake and it dries up, then the sounds it makes go too. The familiar rush of a waterfall might be central to a people's legends and history. The sounds of insects, birds and animals that live near water are an important part of their sense of place.

To the south of Peterborough there used to be a lake called Whittlesea Mere. It formed when parts of the River Nene silted up in around 500BC and water couldn't escape downriver. The floods formed into lagoons and eventually became a single shallow lake up to six miles long. It was the largest lake in lowland England and a rich habitat for wildlife. People used it to hunt for birds and fish, and to harvest the reeds used in thatching. There was a wide range of plants, and John Clare walked there from Helpston to study rare ferns. It was also used for pleasure boating and regattas in the summer, and for ice-skating competitions in winter.

The Mere survived for more than two millennia because it was low-lying and difficult to drain. But in 1851 a channel was dug and a steam pump started to remove the water. It was gone in a matter of weeks. The sounds of wildfowl will have drained away too as the area became farmland. The large copper butterflies that thrived in the fen habitat became extinct. A post was driven into the ground at Holme Fen to see how much the peat would shrink after the Mere was drained. The top of the post started out level with the topsoil. Today it protrudes more than twelve feet above ground. It's officially the lowest place in England. The area has been literally hollowed out.

6 DECEMBER: Today I see something that makes me a bit less confident about the future of the local kingfishers. I watch aghast as one flies over the top of the bridge then dodges in and out of the speeding cars. It travels fast and zigzags, but it is only just above the level of the roofs. I don't like to think what would happen if it tries to dodge a large lorry.

Kingfishers have been known to live for more than four years, but it's estimated that three out of four adults die each year. Traffic accidents cause some of that, as do collisions with glass windows on houses near rivers and streams. Cats can catch the birds when they perch near garden ponds, stoats and weasels may enter their nests, and sparrowhawks hunt them in the open. Flooded waters make catching fish harder, and ice can make it impossible. Pollution may reduce the numbers of fish and cause a build-up of harmful chemicals or disruptive hormones in both predator and prey. And many of the youngsters never learn to fish properly, and can even drown in the attempt.

The mortality figures are offset by the large number of chicks that a pair can hatch in a year, but they give some idea of the fine balances involved in a species' survival.

7 DECEMBER: I meet Neil by the river this morning. He lives locally and spends a lot of time walking and photographing wildlife. When we bump into each other we share tips and experiences. He tells me about a trip he made to the Masai Mara in Kenya. Later in the day he sends me a photo he took there of a grey-headed kingfisher. It is easily recognisable as a kingfisher, even though there is just a thin line of blue along the edges of its wings. The body shape and feet are the same, and it has a long-pointed beak, albeit bright orange and thicker at the base.

Kingfishers are part of a larger order of birds called Coraciiformes which includes rollers, todies, motmots and bee-eaters. They're usually very colourful, and nest in holes and cavities. They range considerably in size. Todies can be just a few inches long while hornbills can have a five-foot wingspan. But the main thing that places them in the same part of the evolutionary tree is the structure of their toes. They're generally syndactyl, which means that three toes point forward and the two outer toes are fused together.

There are other tiny details to do with the shape of their palate bones and inner ears that have helped scientists to distinguish kingfishers as a separate family, but new advances in DNA mean that classifications are always being refined. When Rosemary Eastman's book was published in 1966 there were thought to be eighty-four living species of kingfishers. Today the number has risen to nearer a hundred and twenty, and that may rise still further as research continues.

Many types of kingfishers eat fish and live on rivers. Others don't. The grey-headed variety that Neil spotted in Kenya feeds on insects and lizards. Another member of the family is the kookaburra, a large Australian bird with a famous laughing call. It lives in trees and feeds on mice, snakes and small reptiles. Its beak has adapted to be shorter and stronger to deal with its prey and habitat.

9 DECEMBER: It's the second frosty day in a row, and parts of the canal by the bridge have frozen over. A charm of goldfinches flits down the riverbank in front of me. They land now and again to sway on the teasels. I spot a green woodpecker in a tree. It flies down into the white frosted grass and picks at the hard earth. Every now and again I can see a big round eye as its sharp beak comes up and points to the sky.

On the way back the air begins to warm. The willows throw long, thin frost shadows across the meadow.

10 DECEMBER: As I walk along a public footpath this afternoon, I can hear gunfire and rough male voices. The sheep in the field by the

river are running about in panic, and some square up and butt one other. As I come closer, I see about twenty shooters standing in a line, blasting pheasants that are being driven into the air by beaters. One stands with his gun right on the path. Another is about thirty yards further into the field. As a bird flies over he swivels round and fires directly above where I will soon be walking.

I keep going. It is as if I've stumbled into a black-magic ritual where the unsmiling participants are so intent on what they're doing that they've not even noticed me. There is nobody keeping watch for walkers. When I reach the man on the path I ask if it is legal to shoot from there. He ignores me.

I look up the legal situation when I get home. Surprisingly, you can shoot from a public footpath, though not within fifty feet of a road. It's recommended that there are lookouts for passers-by but it doesn't appear to be a requirement. The law seems more concerned that no shot should fall onto a neighbouring owner's land.

13 DECEMBER: I need to get away for a day and feel drawn downriver to the wide skies of the Fens. I've been reading a book by Edward Storey called *The Solitary Landscape*. Born and bred in Whittlesey, he wrote with great feeling and poetry about the fen country around his home. There's a passage in the book about walking the north bank of the Nene between Peterborough and Whittlesey. I decide to go there and experience it for myself.

I drive to Peterborough and park on an embankment near the imposing Norman cathedral. The town is thirty miles from the sea, but the river was still tidal here until 1937. I set out to walk a few miles downriver to the lock that was built to control the seawaters.

Behind me I can hear the distant hoots of a steam train whistling along the Nene Valley Railway on the far side of town.

The river is dead straight and raised up above the surrounding land. The path is on top of an embankment, so it's easy to walk and take in the whole of the landscape at the same time. Four wind turbines tower over the meadows to the south. There's barely a breeze, and the blades on three of them are still. The fourth turns slowly and deliberately like the second hand on a giant clock. A trail of brown smoke drifts out horizontally from the tip of a factory chimney at the brickworks. A small diesel train rattles along an embankment towards Ely. An ancient biplane drones overhead.

A walker coming towards me stops and points out some fallow deer standing in the undergrowth on the north side of the river. He mentions that he often sees a kingfisher near the sewage works just downstream. When I get there the treated water is discharging into a drainage dyke that's a haven for ducks, including mallards and pochards.

The path meets a road which runs along the riverbank. Edward Storey lamented the growth of traffic there in the 1970s. Now it's like a racetrack, but I'm able to walk up onto a separate embankment and zone it out. From here I'm looking north across the cultivated fens. The peaty black soil shows between rows of bright green seedlings. A huge flock of geese feeds on a field in the distance. A kestrel watches from a telephone pole. I'm standing about twenty feet up on the bank and there's nothing to give me a sense of scale. I could be a giant looking down onto a miniature landscape.

There are scattered farm buildings, but few trees. In many ways this is a strange landscape, shaped and tamed by industrial agriculture. The flat land's been reclaimed from the sea and floodwater but there's still a coastal beauty in the wide sky and the uncertain misty horizon. Flag Fen, the site of the Bronze Age causeway that I visited back in March, isn't far from here. There's no one in my line of sight now, but this land was a home and workplace for people living a very different life for thousands of years.

I reach the Dog-in-a-Doublet lock, named after the pub sited next to it. I sit on a low concrete embankment and drink from a flask. Every now and then there are loud gurgles as water is pumped up into the main river from a drainage dyke below. I'm looking across washes that are flooded in winter and still used for ice skating when there's a run of hard frosts. In the past there were serious competitions with prizes of money and food.

I walk further downriver to Eldernell, where there are more open washes that attract common cranes and short-eared owls. Just as I get there a kingfisher lands in a hawthorn bush. It immediately takes off again when a blackbird lands on the same branch. Two barn owls swoop out of the window opening of an abandoned farm building.

When I get back to the north bank, dusk is falling fast. It's difficult to tell land from sky. Storey felt that there were conflicting forces at work here. The fields once belonged to the floods and saltwater. The sea is forever trying to return. A skein of geese flies over. In the throb of their wingbeats I can sense the ebb and flow of an estuary.

14 DECEMBER: A run of a few mild days has done wonders for the local birds, and there may be new arrivals from other places too. Dawn and dusk are full of the edgy cluck of blackbirds. They

squabble in the hedgerows and gobble red berries with their bright yellow beaks. There are redwings by the bridge this morning, families of goldfinches and a pair of chaffinches. Great tits have begun their full spring song, and at the edge of the wood this morning a song thrush was practising his scales.

15 DECEMBER: I'm walking in Glapthorn Cow Pastures. It's late afternoon. A chatter of fieldfares takes to the sky as I follow the path through the oak trees. I stop for a moment to listen to the strong wind in their branches, then walk up the gentle slope between the ash trees. Near the western edge of the wood the low sun flickers through the swaying brown and black outlines of trunks and branches. At the top the sky and clouds are blue, grey and pink. Below, the sun is burning copper. In the field beyond, large oaks are picked out in gold from the hedgerows. It's a living, moving, stained-glass window.

Rooks pour into the trees above. ◀》 12.42 They're loud and raucous to begin with, then settle to silence as the colours fade to dusk. I turn and make my way along the muddy path, eyes wide in the dark. At the edge of the wood there are farmhouse lights twinkling on the far side of the valley. A red light moves slowly in the sky above them. I'm unsure what it is at first, then hear the quiet drone of a distant light aircraft. The sound rises and falls as it passes. A tawny owl hoots behind me. Another answers close by. The wind hums in the trees overhead.

17 DECEMBER: I feel the pull to travel downriver again this morning. This time I drive all the way to the mouth of the Nene near Sutton Bridge in Lincolnshire. I want to visit the lighthouse

on the east bank of the river where Peter Scott began his career as a wildlife painter and conservationist. I am also curious to go there because of a book I read when I was nine years old.

Mum and Dad were both great readers, and she used to buy boxes of books at jumble sales. One day I fished out a blue hardback volume with a picture of a flying bird on its cover. Inside, there were painted illustrations of sea and sky, and a portrait of a young woman holding a goose in her arms.

It didn't look like a children's book, but I started to read the words and was pulled into a story about a village girl who brings an injured goose to a strange disfigured loner, an artist called Philip Rhayader, who lives in a lighthouse. I didn't understand every word but was completely caught up in it. I remember gazing into the eerie landscape of the paintings and being devastated by the sad ending when Rhayader was killed in his small boat during the Dunkirk evacuation.

The book was *The Snow Goose* by Paul Gallico. Though the plot was fictional and set in the Essex marshes, the author wrote the story after hearing about Peter Scott's life at Sutton Bridge lighthouse during the 1930s. Scott provided all the paintings and drawings that added so much to the atmosphere of the text.

When I get to the estuary, the river is wide and tidal. Cargo ships and commercial fishing boats travel up it to the Port of Wisbech, and there is a strong smell of silt and creosote. The sky reminds me of Scott's paintings. It is mid-afternoon, and the sun is bringing out mauve and gold highlights in the low clouds offshore. A half-moon hangs in a pale blue sky over the fields inland. I hear an unfamiliar sound and look up. A skein of pink-footed geese flies down the river and out to sea.

The lighthouse is shorter than I expected. It's about the height of a traditional windmill and has simple white outhouses built on to it. Brent geese are standing and swimming in a pond nearby. Scott came here after he left Cambridge and was wondering what to do with his life. He started to paint more seriously and became interested in researching geese rather than simply hunting them. He went away to fight in World War II and came back determined to continue his work with wildlife. Changes made to the sea wall during the war meant the area round the lighthouse was no longer so attractive to geese. Scott chose instead to base his work at Slimbridge, at the mouth of the River Severn in Gloucestershire.

I leave the lighthouse and walk along the sea wall towards the Wash. The tide is ebbing. There are wide stretches of scrubby marsh before the sea's edge, and a little egret flies slowly back and forth across them like a barn owl. There are huge flocks of lapwings on the distant shore, and I can hear curlews and oystercatchers. I stand and gaze across the estuary as the sun goes down. I've imagined this scene for a long time, and it doesn't disappoint. And importantly, as an adult, I can now see that *The Snow Goose* was a work of fiction. That lifts some of the sadness I felt when reading it as a child who didn't yet understand the distinction between stories and the real world.

18 DECEMBER: I'm still seeing a kingfisher by the bridge every day. I think it must be the same one each time because it has a habit of perching high up in a tree before it dives. Sometimes it sits on the guttering of the Wharf House and peers down from there. Unlike other kingfishers, it routinely takes a shortcut across the meadow to reach the main river.

Because it perches so high up it tends to fly over the bridge rather than under it. I've begun to get used to watching it fly through the traffic.

21 DECEMBER: It's the morning of the shortest day, the Solstice, the first day of winter. Robins sing in the garden at first light. A crow calls overhead. Blackbirds cluck against each other in little bursts of different lengths. Sometimes there are two clucks, then three, four or even five. As I walk along the river a song thrush lights up the wood with his song.

In the garden at twilight a single blackbird starts to sing. I've been hoping to hear one for a while, and after a few false alarms from starlings there is no mistaking that lovely mellow tone. It is the first I've heard since summer, and I am spellbound. He only sings for a few minutes but I feel hugely uplifted. There always seems to be an increase in birdsong around the winter solstice. It's almost as if the birds are anticipating the lighter days to come.

23 DECEMBER: I'm standing on the bridge. A kingfisher takes off from one of the metal brackets just below me. It perches in the trees for a while then comes back towards the bridge and flies across the road. There's no traffic apart from a single cyclist. The bird whizzes in front of him. He looks across to me with a big grin and shouts out as he passes: "Wow! Nice kingfisher!"

25 DECEMBER: During nearly a year of thinking about kingfishers I've never dreamed about them, or at least not that I remember. But last night I did, and I recall it very clearly.

I'm in a museum and the building's closed. It's dark, and I'm lying on a bed in the Ancient Egyptian gallery. There are carved stone friezes on the walls around me. One of the walls opens to the outside world. The night's warm and humid. I can hear the lap of waves and the calls of kingfishers. I lie there listening, enjoying the sounds and trying to work out how many birds are calling and how far away they are. Then I wake up back in my own bed with the number 327 at the front of my mind.

The context of the dream isn't entirely surprising. I've been reading about carvings of kingfishers on some Egyptian friezes, and that Egyptians may have believed that the birds' underground nests were a bridge between this world and the afterlife. But I am intrigued by the number 327. I look it up to see if it has any meaning. It seems to foretell new chapters in life, increased energy and freedom from procrastination. That seems all to the good. I also can't help noticing that 327 adds up to twelve, which is the number of months I've been following the kingfishers.

27 DECEMBER: I decide to drive west on the back road towards Uppingham and park near the top of a long, steep hill that runs down into the village of Harringworth. It marks the watershed between the River Nene and the Welland. I walk along a footpath called the Jurassic Way, which is an ancient drover's road that was used for driving flocks of animals on foot from one place to another. It follows a limestone ridge for ninety miles between Stamford in Lincolnshire and Banbury in Oxfordshire.

I stop and look down towards Harringworth. The river passing through the village was used to carry goods, including building stone, at a time when there were no reliable roads. Then in 1878 a spectacular brick viaduct was built to take the railway across the valley. It's the longest in the UK and contains thirty million bricks. At the time it would have been a high-water mark of technical progress, but it's barely used now. Not far away is Corby, a former steel manufacturing town. I remember decades ago seeing the 'Corby Candle', a giant flame that came from a chimney at the steelworks. That's all gone too.

Things change. I look up at a passenger jet trailing its booming roar and vapour trail across the sky. Might people travel less in future? Could quieter electric engines be developed? That's already happening with cars, and lorries could soon become less noisy too. A raven flies over with its croaking call, adding a touch of the prehistoric and reminding me that birds achieved the pinnacle of flight long before humans even started thinking about it. It's also a reminder of more recent changes. Ravens weren't heard in central and eastern England forty years ago. They'd been wiped out after years of persecution by farmers and gamekeepers. Now they're protected by legislation and making a comeback on their own. The fact that I usually hear one when I come out this way is proof that things can change for the better. Red kites and chequered skipper butterflies have been reintroduced within miles of here. There's still hope for wildlife.

29 DECEMBER: This morning in the wood there is a sound I've not heard before. It is a low, guttural '*glunkk*', almost like a low note on an African wooden xylophone. It has to be another raven. I run out of the trees just in time to see it fly across the fields. I return to the wood and pick up a stick from the ground, then start to strike fallen tree trunks and branches, trying to imitate that sound. A robin starts a noisy protest, and I stop straight away. Then a great

spotted woodpecker drums a short burst from a tree in the distance, and I grin from ear to ear.

31 DECEMBER: It's late afternoon on the last day of the year. As I walk along the river I imagine there's a kingfisher on every perch. They glint and gleam in the sun. I can hear their calls, the whirr of wings and the soft sounds as they dive in the water. I feel like I'm part of the story of the river, but there's always a bend ahead. I can never be sure what's round it, nor what the future holds for the river itself. This is a lovely area to live in, but housebuilding and the growing population threaten the quality of the water. The kingfishers may be thriving, but we're not making it easy for them.

I think about the books I've read and the characters I've encountered during this past year. Gilbert White, the eighteenth-century parson with his intensely local observations and insight into ecology. John Clare with his love of the countryside and horror of the changes brought about by modernisation and greed. Lord Lilford, collecting and researching birds on his country estate. The Rothschilds, with their interest in insects and the broader need for conservation. BB, who introduced both children and adults to the countryside through his stories and nature writing. Ludwig Koch, who brought birdsong into people's homes through his recordings and BBC broadcasts. Ronald and Rosemary Eastman, with their nature films. And Peter Scott, who brought the question of the survival of species to worldwide attention.

They were all driven by curiosity and a love of wildlife in its many forms, and they were also aware of just how fragile it could be. Even in his remote country parish three centuries ago Gilbert White could hear the sounds of ships firing guns near Portsmouth and smell the smoke from London sixty miles away. And it's not just famous naturalists that have made a difference. The RSPB and Wildlife Trusts have armies of supporters and volunteers who passionately believe in helping wildlife.

On the way back home I stop on the bridge and look downriver. It's the last sunset of the year. Geese are flying high across the meadows and a grey heron skims low and lands on the far bank. I feel euphoric, like it's the end of term. This year's taught me more than I could ever have imagined about the wildlife, history and culture of the river valley, and about the people who have cared for and conserved it. It's opened up my eyes and ears and stirred up deep feelings of belonging. The turn of the year is a time to look back and count blessings, but also to look forward and pray they'll extend into the future. And it's also a time to take nothing for granted.

There's very little light left now, but there appears to be a small dark shape whizzing across the last reflections of the sky on the water. I take one last look out across the meadows towards the gentle hills beyond, then turn and set off back across the bridge. As I walk, my slow, light footsteps pick up the rhythm of *Kingfisher Blue*, the song I wrote back in the spring:

> *Kingfisher blue, I came looking for you*
> *Brilliant blue, lit up by the sun*
> *You called as you flew, kingfisher blue*
> *And you and the river were one*
> *You and the river were one...*

ACKNOWLEDGMENTS

Many people gave help and advice while I was writing this book, including: Faradena Afifi, Elena Aragonés, Liz Bayliss, Sue Carverhill, Bob Cheatham, Kerry Devine, Barny Dillarstone, Jeremy Hunter, Neil St John, Paul Kirkpatrick, Derek Paice, the Pepper family, Graham Rice, Philip Rudkin, Jonathan Theobald, and Liz and Huw Williams. Thanks are also due to Claire Strange and Anna Moores at Bradt, to Jasmine Parker for the cover, and to James Lowen for his skilled and sympathetic work as both editor and naturalist. My agent Jennifer Barclay was involved with the book from the start and always provided wise and good-humoured help and guidance. I'd also like to thank my mother Pearl for a childhood full of books and reading, and my wife Eleanor for all her love and encouragement during the lengthy ups and downs of the writing process.

READING

This is a small sample of some of the books mentioned in the text, and others that have inspired me in different ways.

J.A. Baker, *The Peregrine*. William Collins, 2017.
H.E. Bates, *Down the River*. Victor Gollancz, 1979.
BB, *A Summer on the Nene*. Kaye And Ward, 1967.
Annie Dillard, *Pilgrim at Tinker Creek*. Harper and Row, 1974.
Rosemary Eastman, *The Kingfisher*. Collins, 1969.
Kenneth Grahame, *The Wind in the Willows*. Fontana, 1983.
Edward Grey, *The Charm of Birds*. Hodder and Stoughton, 1927.
Ludwig Koch, *Memoirs of a Birdman*. Phoenix House, 1955.
Bernie Krause, *Wild Soundscapes: Discovering the Voice of the Natural World*. Wilderness Press, 2002.
Peter Scott, *The Eye of the Wind*. Hodder and Stoughton, 1966.
Edward Storey, *The Solitary Landscape*. Victor Gollancz, 1975.
Gilbert White, *The Natural History of Selborne*. Oxford University Press, 2013

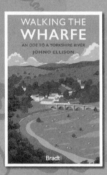

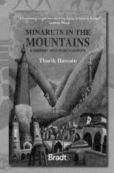
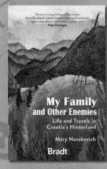

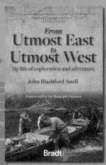

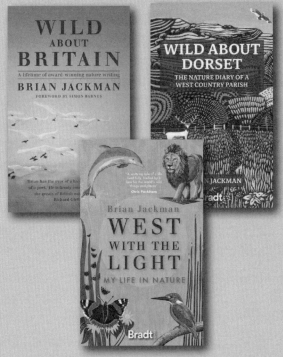